CRAFTSMEN IN BUSINESS:
A Guide to Financial Management and Taxes

by HOWARD W. CONNAUGHTON, C.P.A.

a publication of the AMERICAN CRAFTS COUNCIL

ISBN: 0-88321-016-9

Library of Congress Catalog Card No.: 75-27315

Printed in the United States of America

American Crafts Council
44 West 53 Street
New York, N.Y. 10019

Designed by Emil Antonucci

Howard W. Connaughton began his accounting career in 1926 with the firm of Price, Waterhouse & Company which he served in various capacities until 1944. Prior to establishing his own account-ing firm in 1949 he was Controller and Office Manager of Life Savers Corporation in Port Ches-ter, New York. Since the early 1950s he has been the independent accountant for the American Crafts Council.

The American Crafts Council was founded in 1943 to stimulate interest in contemporary crafts. As a national membership and nonprofit organization it maintains the Museum of Contemporary Crafts in New York City and publishes the bimonthly magazine *Craft Horizons*. Through its Re-gional Program and Research & Education Department the Council is involved in varied educa-tional programs including the national slide-film service "Your Portable Museum." Membership in the Council is open to all. The Council headquarters are at 44 West 53rd Street, New York, New York 10019.

Introduction

"Craftsmen in Business" was conceived as a revision of "Taxes and the Craftsman," a pamphlet published by the American Crafts Council in 1964. It was felt, however, that the subject of taxes should be considerably expanded and other topics on finances added. A totally new publication emerged in the process of broadening the earlier work.

By becoming more informed about financial matters including taxes, the craftsman provides himself with greater control of his business and its future. It is the intent of this book to provide essential information to make this possible, both for the craftsman established in business and others who wish to start a new business.

While this book covers many aspects of financial management, it is not meant to replace the counsel of a qualified accountant or lawyer. Seeking professional help when it is needed is an important point to remember. Another is that tax regulations—federal, state, and local—are subject to change. This book reflects current regulations at the time of publication, but these are likely to alter in future.

We are appreciative to Howard W. Connaughton, who in addition to authorship, assisted the American Crafts Council for many years as its independent accountant.

Lois Moran, *Director*
Research & Education Department
American Crafts Council

CONTENTS

1 GOING INTO BUSINESS FOR YOURSELF

There are many reasons why you may want to go into business for yourself. Perhaps you want to be unrestricted in what you do or make, particularly when you are a craftsman. Another consideration may be taxes, and every craftsman should have some knowledge of this subject.

For federal income tax purposes, as well as for many state taxes, all income that you receive is taxed unless it is expressly exempt by law. You must pay tax on all income you receive from wages, fees, capital gains, interest on your savings, dividends on stock investments, etc. Income you receive from your avocation must also be included in your tax return.

Strictly personal expenses are not deductible against income. Such expenses include repairs, insurance, rent for your apartment or house, and commutation costs (traveling to and from your principal place of work). However, as you will see in a subsequent chapter, certain of these expenses can be deductible if you are in business.

Tax Advantages for Professional Activities

When your avocation is a personal non-professional activity, you may deduct the expenses applicable thereto, but only to the extent of the income you receive from that avocation, and provided that you keep proper records. However, when your avocation is *a profession and you are in business*, you may deduct all ordinary and necessary expenses, even when such expenses exceed your income.

The following example should make this clear. Philips receives $1,000 from the sale of ceramics which he makes at home. He does not operate as a professional. His avocation expenses are $1,800, and he is in the 20% tax bracket. He must report the entire $1,000 of avocation income on his return. Although his expenses are $1,800, since he is a non-professional he can only deduct $1,000.

Jones also receives $1,000 from the sale of ceramics which he makes at home, and his expenses are $1,800. However, he operates as a professional, even though he works at home. As a professional he can deduct the entire $1,800. Jones has other income and is in the 20% tax bracket. Since he deducts $800 more than Philips, he pays $160 less tax ($800 x 20%).

The actual amount in dollars you can save for a deduction will vary according to your tax bracket. If you are in the 20% bracket, a $500 deduction will save you $100. However, if you are in the 40% tax bracket, the same $500 deduction will save you $200.

By making your avocation a profession, you can:

1. deduct those personal expenses applicable to your profession plus all your ordinary and necessary expenses (many of which are not deductible by the non-professional);
2. deduct your losses—expenses in excess of income against other income such as wages, interest, etc.

What Is a Professional Activity?

A profession is that to which you devote your time, attention and labor in order to make a profit or livelihood. The taxing authorities have frequently ruled that an individual may engage in more than one profession, trade or business. Thus you may hold a regular job or operate a business and still have a second profession—your avocation. To you the second profession is a sideline, but that does not prevent you from taking a professional's tax advantages.

It is not enough for you simply to assert that your avocation is a profession. You must also be able to prove this to the tax authorities who may require evidence that such an activity does not come under the classification of a hobby.

According to Section 183 of the Internal Revenue Code, in order to be considered in business and not to be operating as a hobby (an activity not engaged in for profit), you must show a profit in two out of five consecutive years. Therefore, it is most important that you do everything you can to make a profit, at least a small one, particularly in the first two years. It might not be easy, but with some sales and good planning it can be done. If you succeed in this, then if called upon, you should not have any difficulty in establishing the fact that you are in business.

If you fail to make a profit in two out of five consecutive years, that does not necessarily mean that you are not engaged in the activity for profit. Failing to meet this test means only that the taxpayer has the burden of proof, which will not occur unless his return is examined.

If, after an examination of your return, the Internal Revenue Service should say that you are not in business but are engaged in a hobby, then the burden of proof is on you. The above provision also applies to individual proprietorships, partnerships, and individuals who are part of what is known as a Subchapter S corporation, but not to other corporation taxpayers.

The tax authorities will regard your intent as expressed by your acts. They will not be primarily interested in your subjective intent, but in your intent as it appears from your activities.

The following guidelines should be followed if you wish to be classified as a professional:

1. Your primary purpose for engaging in your activities should be to make a financial profit. Investing capital will give substantiating evidence of your profit motive.
2. Keep complete accounting records of your income and expenses. Your records should be as detailed as possible, as will be explained later.
3. If possible, maintain a separate bank account for your professional activities.
4. Use printed stationery, business cards, invoices, etc.
5. Obtain a professional listing in the telephone directory.
6. Give your activity your personal attention. This will show your serious intention to conduct your activity as a professional rather than for pure pleasure. The fact that you enjoy your work does not make it any less a profession.
7. A few isolated transactions are not sufficient to classify your activities as a profession. You must show that you have been operating over a period of time and that you plan to continue operating in the future.

To qualify as a professional you need not meet all of the above requirements, but the more you meet, the stronger your position will be should the Treasury Department question your professional status. At the very minimum you must:

1. intend to make a profit;
2. show that your efforts are directed at making a profit;
3. separate your personal expenses and income from your professional expenses and income;
4. maintain detailed books and records.

Whether your activities are professional or personal will depend on the particular facts of your situation. You might start by comparing your activities with those of the taxpayers in the following actual cases in which they tried to convince the court that they were professionals and thus should be permitted to deduct their losses.

1. A prominent social and civic leader, with a large income from independent sources, produced 500 paintings and sold 50. Her painting expenses were 18 times greater than the income from her activities. However, she refused to accept purchase offers at amounts less than she considered necessary to maintain her prestige as an artist. The court held that she did not intend to

conduct her activities as a professional but rather as an amateur, and thus she could not deduct expenses in excess of her income.

2. A sculptor held exhibitions and offered his work for sale to the public. The court held that he was a professional and could deduct his losses.

3. For years a photographer operated a studio where he took portraits. He also took outdoor photographs. After he closed his studio, he continued his photographic work from his house. He made field trips to national parks where he made films and still shots. He toured the country illustrating his lectures with these photographs. His equipment was of the kind used by professionals rather than amateurs. He convinced the court that photography was his profession and that he intended to make a profit. The court held that his losses were deductible.

4. In a recent decision, the court held that losses incurred by a photographer were deductible inasmuch as they were incurred in the operation of a photography business for profit. The defendant was able to establish that she was seriously involved in her profession, that she had made sales of her photographs commercially, and that she had received income from presenting her slides to audiences. A good part of her loss in the years in question was from expenses in traveling to Africa in pursuit of her profession.

These four cases demonstrate that the Internal Revenue Service will not hesitate to question whether a person's activity is personal or professional. Be prepared to substantiate your deductions and follow the guidelines laid down in this book.

Not all professions or businesses make a profit from their inception. The fact that you lose money at the outset or over a period of time does not in itself mean that you do not intend to make a profit. Just keep in mind that for your activity to be classified as a profession you must show a profit in two out of five consecutive years. However, as mentioned previously, when filing federal income tax returns as an individual or as a member of a Subchapter S corporation you may deduct your losses when:

1. the profit motive was one of the main reasons you began your activity;
2. you believe that your activity will eventually become profitable.

As mentioned previously, failing to make a profit in two out of five consecutive years does not necessarily mean that you are not engaged in the activity for profit. However, should your return be examined, then the burden of proof

is on you.

To be in business, you as a craftsman must produce and sell what you have made, manage your time and assets, account for your income, expenses and capital expenditures, and prepare and file tax returns with the federal, state and local authorities.

Production

Before you can succeed in any business, you must have a product that you can make from obtainable materials and for which there is a market. There are three basic cost elements involved in your product: materials, labor, and overhead. Each in itself is important.

First, you must select materials that are available, so that once you design your product you can obtain those materials from a supplier within a reasonable time and at a price you can afford.

Next, you must consider the time and labor needed to make the product. If it is an item that only you as a craftsman can create, you alone know what time you have available for production. If you need people to assist you, then you must decide whether the type of help you need is available at a price you can afford to pay.

Finally, there is the important consideration of your overhead, or the cost of running your shop or studio. This includes the rent to be paid for your studio, or a portion of your costs for an apartment or house if you don't wish to have a separate studio. If your plans include such an outside rental, then you should contact a reliable real estate agent to help you find something suitable at a price you can afford to pay, remembering that besides basic rent there will be other costs, such as electricity and heat if they are not a part of your landlord's charge for rent.

In addition, there are the tools, machinery, and equipment that you must use—for example, the wheel that you use in making pottery, the kiln, the workbench, the storage unit for your materials, etc. These will become a part of your cost through what is known as depreciation. Depreciation, in simple terms, means writing off your costs over an allowable period of time. This subject is covered extensively in Chapter 6.

Other costs would include fire insurance to protect you against loss, workmen's compensation insurance, packing and shipping materials, and taxes applicable to production, such as payroll taxes for your employees. You may also have other expenses for cleaning supplies, trash removal, janitorial service, repairs to equipment, etc. Thus many items will enter into what makes up the cost of your product. The bookkeeping necessary for maintaining a record of these costs is discussed in subsequent chapters.

Selling

When you are finally ready to sell your finished product, you must first determine the price you will charge so that you will make a profit, having taken into consideration all of the costs involved in its production, plus your estimated selling and administrative expenses.

For the craftsman there are numerous outlets for sales. Many retail stores specialize in crafts, as do galleries, gift shops and department stores. In recent years, craft fairs have become popular and afford an opportunity to display, sell, and become acquainted with the buying public.

Your approach to selling will depend in great part on the type of product you develop. Design considerations are most important in achieving a product that will appeal to prospective buyers. Well thought out approaches to marketing a product are also essential. Guidance on selling and conducting a business can be found in various printed references. The American Crafts Council publishes an annotated bibliography, "Crafts as Business," which may be ordered through its Publication Department.

Before you can sell a product you must arrive at a fair sales price—fair to yourself considering the time and talent put into the product. Naturally the price you charge should be sufficient to recover the direct costs of materials, labor and overhead, as well as your selling and administrative expenses, and enable you to make a profit so that you may continue in business. Therefore, it is essential for you to keep good records, and this point is covered extensively in subsequent chapters.

The determination of a fair price can be affected by other factors such as competition, supply and demand, design, and the utility value of the product. If your product is unique, then in a sense you have no competition, and thus if your product is useful and/or desirable, you can afford to charge a higher price.

As always, supply and demand play a most important part in determining a fair sales price. If your product has a very limited market, there would be little point in producing it in large quantities. By the same token, if there are many products that resemble yours, then your sales possibilities may be limited unless yours is just a little bit different or better.

Management

Management in a broad sense is ensuring that your business is run properly and economically. It includes not only making decisions in regard to production, sales and other policy matters but also having capable employees or outside consultants for those phases of business in which you need help.

One such area would be insurance. It is important to insure your assets against fire, theft, etc., and thus you should know what types of insurance are available and desirable and what type of company—stock or mutual—best suits your needs. For this you should consult a reliable insurance agent or broker. In addition, if you have employees you must carry workmen's compensation and disability insurance in some states. Product liability insurance is still another consideration. Your insurance man will be able to advise you on these matters.

There are many other fields in which you may need professional help as your business grows. Among these are advertising, sales promotion, and accounting and tax services.

For your own protection, if you plan to employ people to assist you, you should be generally familiar with any state and federal regulations regarding employees, such as minimum wages and working conditions. Data pertaining to such regulations can be obtained from federal and state government offices in your area that deal with labor.

If you want to use a name for your operations other than your own, you may be required to register with your county clerk's office and pay a nominal fee. As a general rule, when you open a business bank account in that name, it is necessary to have an extra copy of this registration form, which can be obtained at the same time you register.

Naturally, there are advantages and disadvantages to each form of business organization. For the corporation, the basic attributes are: when its name is approved it can hold property and make contracts; it can be sued, or sue, in that name; its continued existence within the limits of the articles of incorporation affords limited liability for its stockholders, who except in special cases are not liable for its debts and obligations beyond the amount of full paid capital. Of course in a corporation, upon compliance with certain rules and regulations, you can provide a pension or profit-sharing agreement for yourself and your employees.

Should you wish to operate as a corporation, then you must employ an attorney familiar with corporations and their procedures to carry you through the legal steps. You will also have to file an income tax return for the corporation and pay a tax on the profits. You will take a salary for your work, and any distribution of profits to you will be a dividend and be taxed as a dividend. This is what is meant by double taxation—the corporation is taxed on its profits, and then you are taxed on the dividends paid to you.

There is an alternative to this double taxation, however. If your corporation has no more than ten shareholders and meets other conditions, you may file a tax return for its profits or losses under what is known as Subchapter S. In this instance, after making proper election and filing a special form with the Internal Revenue Service, each stockholder will report his share of profits or take his share of losses individually, with the corporation itself paying no federal tax.

Rather than form a corporation, you may wish to join with another person or persons and operate under what is known as a partnership. Here, too, it is advisable to employ an attorney familiar with such matters, to draft an agreement, and to have your accountant review the proposed agreement before it is signed.

Many things should be considered in such an agreement—for example, the division of profits or losses between partners. Moreover, unlike a corporation, if one partner should die, the partnership must either be dissolved and a new one formed, or there must be a sale or liquidation of the assets. As in a single proprietorship, all partners are equally liable for the debts of the partnership unless certain partners are limited by the partnership agreement.

For tax purposes, a partnership files a special information return, since each partner is taxed on his share of the profits as shown in that return. Likewise, if there is a loss, a partner will deduct that loss from any other income he may be reporting on his individual return.

Unless you have a definite person with whom you wish to start a business, the single proprietorship form of business would be better taxwise and less cumbersome. Under this setup you will file what is known as a Schedule C (Form 1040). This is explained more fully in a later chapter. If you operate as a single proprietorship, you are personally liable for its debts. Once your business grows profitwise, you should generally change over to the corporate form of organization, but at the beginning there seems no need to incur the legal expenses involved in setting up a corporation.

Copyrights and Patents

Once you have decided to go into business and believe that you have a saleable product, then the question arises as to how you can stop others from copying your design. Much has been written on this subject, but essentially you can protect yourself by obtaining either a copyright or a patent.

A copyright applies to creative works. If you have a product that may be so classified, a copyright can be obtained easily and inexpensively. All you need to do is to obtain an application form (covering works of art) from the Register of Copyrights, Library of Congress, Washington, D.C. 120559. Complete this form and mail it together with two photographs of your product and a check for $6 to that office. When a copy of your application is returned to you, it will indicate when it was filed, and you can mark your product accordingly. The copyright is good for 28 years and is renewable for 28 more. The fact that you have obtained a copyright might discourage others from copying your design, but it is no guarantee. If someone does copy it and you want to stop him, it generally means that you must take legal action. You must decide whether to do so is worthwhile to safeguard your reputation and also to avert any possible reduction of the future profits you may make. The cost of procuring a copyright is not deductible as an expense, but it is a capital expenditure recoverable by depreciation.

A patent is quite different. To obtain one, your product must be different, original, and your own invention. If your design is a useful product, you cannot obtain a copyright, but you can protect it with a design patent.

Before a patent can be obtained, an application must be filed with the Patent Office where a thorough search is made to assure that no one else has previously obtained a patent on a similar product. A design patent is more expensive to obtain than a copyright, and it is generally advisable to hire an attorney experienced in that field to help you rather than to handle things yourself.

Many people believe that a design patent offers more protection than a copyright, but this is not necessarily so. From a practical standpoint the copyright gives you some protection and is less costly and less difficult to obtain.

When you have an idea for a product that you think will have a good market, it is good business practice not to tell others about it. If you believe that the market is so extensive that you cannot produce your product in sufficient quantities, then perhaps you will be able to locate a manufacturer who will contract to pay you a royalty for the use of your design.

Accounting

Record-keeping can be burdensome, but it is necessary not only to enable you to file proper tax returns but also to guide you in your day-to-day operations as to what products are selling, what your profits are for each product, what your overhead is, etc. Also, your records have an historical value, since they accumulate information from year to year. They will show the cost of your fixed assets such as cameras, machines, or other equipment that you own. The value of these items will be useful in determining the amount of coverage for insurance and form a basis for determining the depreciation expense for accounting and tax purposes.

Basically, accounting involves recording your daily business transactions in journals and ledgers by what is known as a double entry bookkeeping system. This is explained in detail in subsequent chapters.

Taxes

You are required to pay an income tax if your business shows a profit, unless that profit is offset by other losses. There are many types of taxes, but the most familiar are the federal income tax and the various state and city income taxes. Many of those state and city taxes are based on the rules and regulations prescribed by the Internal Revenue Code.

Depending on where your business is located, there may be other business taxes, such as commercial rent taxes and occupancy taxes. It is generally advisable to engage a qualified accountant, at least on a consultant basis, to get you started so that at least you will know what tax forms must be prepared.

2 HOW TO KEEP BOOKS AND RECORDS

Bookkeeping is an art, and like any other art it requires study and practice. There are certain factors that you must keep in mind. For example, a record of each business transaction should be kept—preferably on what is known as the double entry or self-balancing system of bookkeeping, where the total debits must equal the total credits.

An axiom of this system is that assets minus liabilities equal net worth or capital, and that income less expenses is your profit. Naturally if your expenses are greater than your income, then you have a loss.

An asset is something that you own or possess which has value—for example, cash or something that you can turn into cash, such as a debt owed to you (known as an account receivable). On the other hand, a liability is something you owe, such as an amount payable to a creditor or a mortgage on your property. Net worth is just what the term implies. It indicates what your business is worth after you have deducted your losses from the capital you have invested in the business and your profits.

Journals and Ledgers

Bookkeeping involves the maintenance of various journals and ledgers. Journals are used to record your day-to-day transactions, including both cash receipts and cash disbursements. In regard to ledgers, the basic one is the general ledger. This is used to record the amounts shown as columnar totals from the various journals or from summaries of entries of a particular column in a journal.

In addition, there is sometimes a need for a subsidiary ledger, particularly if you sell on credit. If you do, you will have charge accounts, or what is called "Accounts Receivable." The subsidiary ledger will give detailed information in support of what is known as a control account in the general ledger. For example, when you have accounts receivable, the total of the entries from the sales journal is listed under the control account in the general ledger. Then individual postings are made to the accounts maintained for each customer in the subsidiary ledger. The total of all the individual accounts at the end of any accounting period would agree with the balance of the general ledger control account. The principles applied here to Accounts Receivable can also be used in other instances where a subsidiary ledger is needed—for example, accounts payable, inventory, etc.

To make an entry you must have a debit or debits offset in amount by a credit or credits. Such an entry will be recorded as either increasing or decreasing assets, liabilities and net worth. As we shall show, debits may result in (1) increase in an asset, (2) decrease in a liability, (3) decrease in net worth, (4) increase in an expense, or (5) decrease in income, while credits may result in the opposite, that is, (1) decrease in an asset, (2) increase in a liability, (3) increase in net worth, (4) decrease in an expense, or (5) increase in income.

For example, suppose that Craftsman A starts in business and invests $1,000. He plans for the present to operate as a sole proprietor. The entry in a cash receipts book or journal would be:

1. Debit: Cash $1,000.00
       Credit: Craftsman A, Capital $1,000.00

Note: To assist you in getting a quick understanding of the transactions, these entries are being set up in journal entry form. Actually they would be recorded in columnar journals, as explained later on.

Cash is an asset and the debit would increase it, which in this instance starts or opens the account. Since Capital is a net worth account, the investment of $1,000 would increase this and thus be a credit entry.

Now suppose Craftsman A is a potter and he needs a throwing wheel for his use. Having recently purchased one for $400, he decides to use this in his business rather than buy another one. His entry would be:

2. Debit: Machinery & Equipment $400.00
       Credit: Craftsman A, Capital $400.00

Machinery and equipment are also assets, since they have a life of over one year and are subject to depreciation. Thus the acquisition of the throwing wheel would increase the account and therefore be a debit, while the Capital account is again increased through a credit.

The next step would be to purchase clay, and the entry resulting from this, assuming it is a cash rather than a credit purchase, would be:

3. Debit: Materials $100.00
       Credit: Cash $100.00

We would debit Materials, thus increasing an expense account, and credit Cash, decreasing an asset account.

If the purchase was made on credit, the entry would be:

Debit: Materials $100.00
       Credit: Accounts Payable Trade $100.00

The entry to the Materials expense account remains the same; however, we credit Accounts Payable—Trade, because we are increasing a liability account.

Craftsman A could make other expenditures such as the following:

4. Debit: Rent $100.00
           Stationery and Office Supplies $ 20.00
           Shipping Supplies $ 80.00
    Credit: Cash $200.00

Here again, the entries are similar to the purchase of materials in that we are debiting, or increasing expense accounts, and crediting Cash and reducing an asset account.

Now, suppose Craftsman A completes a pot and sells it to a retail shop for cash. To record this sale the entry would be:

5. Debit: Cash $300.00
    Credit: Sales $300.00

He has received cash, and therefore Cash would be debited, since he is increasing an asset; he would also credit Sales, since he has increased an income account.

If the sale had been made on credit, the entry would be:

Debit: Accounts Recievable Trade $300.00
    Credit: Sales $300.00

The entry to Sales would remain the same; however the debit would be to Accounts Receivable—Trade because he is increasing an asset account.

Now let us summarize these entries eliminating those applicable to credit transactions. For the sake of simplicity, we shall use what are called "T" accounts (in essence, ledger accounts) and employ the same numbers as shown in the above entries.

CASH

Debits	Credits
(1) $1,000.00	*(3)* $ 100.00
(5) 300.00	*(4)* 200.00

MACHINERY & EQUIPMENT

Debits	Credits
(2) $ 400.00	

13

RENT

Debits	Credits
(4) $ 100.00	

SHIPPING SUPPLIES

Debits	Credits
(4) $ 80.00	

CRAFTSMAN A, CAPITAL

Debits	Credits
	(1) $1,000.00
	(2) 400.00

MATERIALS

Debits	Credits
(3) $ 100.00	

STATIONERY & OFFICE SUPPLIES

Debits	Credits
(4) $ 20.00	

SALES

Debits	Credits
	(5) $ 300.00

If we now total each account, determine in the case of the cash account the balance, and then summarize these accounts by taking off what is termed a trial balance, we find that there are equal debits and credits, and that our trial balance would be in balance, i.e.:

	Debits	*Credits*
Cash	$1,000.00	
Machinery & Equipment	400.00	
Craftsman A, Capital		$1,400.00
Materials	100.00	
Rent	100.00	
Stationery & Office Supplies	20.00	
Shipping Supplies	80.00	
Sales		300.00
	$1,700.00	$1,700.00

We cannot emphasize too strongly the necessity for keeping accurate records to assist you in the preparation of your tax returns and for evidence in case of an audit. The kind of records you should maintain is not specified by law. However, regardless of the system of bookkeeping you select, your books must contain a systematic record that will accurately and clearly reflect your income, deductions, credits, and any other information that you will be required to report in your tax returns. Memoranda or sketchy records which merely approximate your income, deductions or other pertinent items affecting your tax liability will not be considered adequate for compliance with the law.

To substantiate your deductions as a professional you must maintain permanent records which clearly show income, deductions and credits, inventories, etc.

Retention of Records

You are required by law to keep available at all times the books and records of your business for inspection by Treasury Department officers and other authorities. Records in support of items appearing in your income tax return should in all cases be retained for at least three years after the return is due to be filed.

Since there are many other rules and regulations, a new businessman should retain all of his records for the first several years. In addition, he should engage a qualified accountant at least to prepare or review his tax returns and to provide other professional assistance.

There are many cases in which a taxpayer should retain indefinitely all his records, including invoices to support certain purchases—for example, when you buy or acquire a depreciable asset to be used in your professional work, purchase property such as land or a building, or invest in securities, particularly those which you plan to hold for a long period of time. This type of record or invoice has to be retained so as to support your claims regarding future sales, losses due to fire, etc.

Separate Bank Accounts

To help achieve your goal of keeping accurate records, you should deposit all professional or business receipts in a bank account, preferably a separate one maintained specifically for your business transactions. In addition you should establish a petty cash fund for small expenditures.

Paying for Expenses

Any professional or business expenses paid by cash should be well documented so that you will be able to prove that they were for business purposes. If possible, make all payments by check so that you will have an accurate record of your professional/business expenses. The check will show the payee's or vendor's endorsement and thus serve as a receipt. You should also, if possible, obtain an invoice that describes exactly what you have purchased. This invoice should show the date of purchase, where the material or item was delivered, and the price of each article purchased.

Before you pay an invoice, it should be checked to see that it correctly states the number of items purchased, that the price of each item and the total cost is accurate, and that the sales tax, if any, has been properly added and calculated. In most states, if you purchase something for resale, you should not be charged for sales tax.

Do not write checks payable to yourself unless they are drawn for personal reasons. If you must write a check drawn to cash or to yourself in order to pay a professional or business expense by cash, you should get a receipt and make that receipt for the cash payment a part of your records. If you cannot get a receipt for a cash payment, you should make an adequate explanation in your records at the time of payment.

After each invoice is checked for the receipt of merchandise, mathematical accuracy, etc., the expenditure must be coded or classified according to what was purchased, a liability to be paid or an expense incurred. Thus you must classify your accounts and eventually record the expenditures under the correct accounts.

Chart of Accounts

In order better to accomplish this classification or coding if you don't have an accountant, you should set up your own chart of accounts and consistently follow that classification. Naturally, you can expand your chart at any time, but the main thing is to be consistent—i.e., when you incur the liability for or pay the telephone bill, it is always a debit to telephone expense and should not be shifted from month to month to a different expense account. Consistency will make possible a proper comparison of your accounts month by month and year by year.

It is generally a good idea if your chart is so set up that it will be of assistance to you in the preparation of your federal tax return without additional analysis. You can obtain a sample chart of accounts from any good bank or accountant. However, you may wish to set up your own chart, and therefore we are presenting here a sample chart of accounts which may be expanded or compressed at any time to meet your needs. You will note that each account is numbered; this will permit you to show an account number instead of the name of the account when you are coding entries or invoices. This sample chart shows balance sheet accounts, assets, liabilities and net worth accounts (ownership equity) first, and then accounts for the profit and loss statement or for income and expenses.

Account No.

BALANCE SHEET (Accounts 1 thru 19)

ASSETS (1-6)

Cash (1)
Petty Cash (Cash on hand)	1.1
Cash in Bank (Regular bank account)	1.2

Receivables (2)
Notes Receivable	2.1
Accounts Receivable—Customers	2.2
Accounts Receivable—Others	2.3

Inventories (3)
Inventory—Goods for Sale	3.1
Inventory—Supplies	3.2

17

18

Long Term Obligations (12)
  Notes Payable—Long Term   12.1

OWNERSHIP EQUITY (15)

  *Capital Investment (Investment in business)   15.1
  **Capital Stock (Stock issued)   15.1
  *Drawing (Cash, etc. used personally)   16.1
  Retained Earnings (Profits, less losses)   16.2
  **Dividends Paid   16.3

PROFIT OR LOSS STATEMENT (Accounts 20-90)

Sales and Other Income (20)
  Sales of Merchandise   20.1
  Sales Returns & Allowances   20.2
  Cash Discounts Allowed
    (Discounts to customers)   20.3
  Cash Discounts Taken
    (Discounts from suppliers)   20.4
  Miscellaneous Income   20.5

Cost of Goods Sold (30)
  Material or Merchandise Purchased   30.1
  Manufacturing Supplies   30.2

Operating Expenses (40)
  Wages   40.1
  Other Labor   40.2
  Payroll Taxes   40.3
  Supplies, Shipping, Etc.   40.4
  Tools   40.5
  Rental of Equipment   40.6
  Repairs   40.7
  Truck Maintenance
    (Gas & oil for trucks)   40.8
  Rent & Utilities   40.9
  Taxes—Real Estate   40.10

*For use only by sole owners or partners
**For use only by corporations
**For use by corporations

Selling Expenses (50)

Salaries—Salesmen	50.1
Advertising	50.2
Automobile Expense	50.3
Commissions	50.4
Travel & Entertainment Expense	50.5
Other	50.6

Administrative Expenses (General Expenses) (60)

Salaries (Other)	60.1
Office Supplies, Stationery	60.2
Postage	60.3
Telephone & Telegraph	60.4
Dues & Subscriptions	60.5
Group Insurance	60.6
Insurance—Other	60.7
Legal & Accounting	60.8
Bad Debts	60.9

Miscellaneous Expenses (70)

Interest	70.1

Depreciation (80)

Depreciation	80.1
(Space is shown in account numbers to allow for depreciation expense by type of asset if desired)	
Amortization—Improvements to Leased Premises	80.5

Taxes (90)

**Federal Income Taxes	90.1
**State Income Taxes	90.2

Accounting Methods

A method of accounting is that set of rules under which you ascertain when and how to record income and expenses in your books, and how to prepare a profit and loss statement for your accounting period. Income is not always in the form of cash. It is sufficient that income items and expenditures can be valued in terms of cash.

Taxable income must be computed on the basis of a fixed accounting period and in accordance with a set of rules to determine the time and manner of reporting income and deductions.

You must be consistent and compute taxable income in accordance with a method of accounting regularly used in keeping books, if that method clearly reflects your income. Any method of accounting which reflects the consistent application of generally accepted accounting principles in a profession or business and which is in accordance with accepted conditions or practices in such a profession or business will ordinarily be regarded as clearly reflecting income. A method of accounting does not clearly reflect income unless all items of gross income and all deductions are treated consistently from year to year.

No particular method of accounting is prescribed for all taxpayers. Each should use the system that in his judgment is best suited to his purpose and will enable him to make an accurate record of his true income. Therefore, in addition to your permanent books of account, you should keep whatever other records and data may be required to support the entries on your books and tax returns.

Among the essentials that must be considered in maintaining such records are the following:

1. Inventories are required in all cases where the production, purchase, or sale of merchandise is an income-producing factor.
2. Expenditures must be classified properly as between capital and expense.
3. Any expenditure (other than ordinary repairs) made to restore property or prolong the useful life of a depreciation asset must be charged to the property account or appropriate reserve and not to current expenses.

If you do not use a specific and consistent method of accounting, or if the method you employ does not clearly reflect income, then your income will be computed in accordance with a method which, in the opinion of the Internal Revenue Service, does clearly reflect income.

Subject to the above rules a taxpayer may compute his taxable income under any of the following methods of accounting:

1. Cash receipts and disbursements method.
2. Accrual method.
3. Any other method which clearly reflects your income, including combinations of the above methods (hybrid method).

The *cash receipts and disbursements method* requires you to include in gross income all items of income you *actually* or *constructively* (described below) receive during the year, whether you receive them in cash, property, or services. Property and services received must be included at their fair market value. Generally, expenses must be deducted in the tax year in which they are actually paid.

Expenses paid in advance, however, are generally deductible only in the year to which they apply. Thus, the payment in 1974 for a three-year insurance policy for the years 1974, 1975, and 1976 must be pro-rated over the period the insurance is in effect. If you use the calendar year for accounting and tax purposes and paid $300 on June 30 for the three-year policy, $50 is deductible for the first year, $100 for each of the next two years, and $50 for the last year. Expense supplies which are on hand at the end of the year are not included in inventory but are treated as expenses paid in advance unless such supplies will become a part of goods manufactured and intended for sale.

A *constructive* receipt of income occurs when an amount is credited to your account or is set apart for you (even though it is not actually in your possession) so that it is subject to your control and you may draw upon it at any time. To constitute receipt in such a case, the amount must be available to you without any substantial limitation or restriction as to the time or manner of payment or to the conditions upon which payment is to be made to you. For example, interest credited to your bank account in December 1974 must be included in your gross income for 1974, and not for 1975 when it is withdrawn or entered in your passbook. Checks and other property cannot be held from one year to another to avoid payment of tax on the income, since such income is properly included in the year in which the checks or other property are set aside for you and are subject to your demand.

When you use the *accrual method*, all items of income are included in gross income when earned, even though not received, and allowable expenses are deducted as soon as incurred, whether or not they have been paid.

If inventory is a factor in determining income, only an accrual method of accounting in regard to purchases and sales will correctly reflect your income. Generally if you sell merchandise you must use an accrual method for purchases and sales.

Special methods of accounting are permitted or required for installment and deferred payment sales, long-term contracts, and depreciation.

A combination of methods may be used if it clearly reflects income and is consistently used. This is known as the *hybrid method*. However, as we have previously stated, special treatment of certain items of income and expense must comply with requirements relating to such items.

If you use the cash method in computing gross income from your profession, you must use the cash method for professional expenses. If you use the accrual method for business expenses, you must use the accrual method for all items affecting gross professional income.

Professional and personal items may be accounted for under different methods. Thus, you may compute the income from your profession under an accrual method even though you must use the cash method for personal items.

If you have more than one profession, a different method of accounting may be used for each separate and distinct business, provided that the method used for each clearly reflects the income of each. For example, you may use the cash receipts and disbursements method for a personal service business and an accrual method for a manufacturing business. However, a business is not separate and distinct unless a complete and separate set of books and records is kept for such a business.

Even if not described above, any method of accounting which is consistently followed may be used as long as it clearly reflects income. However, to change your method of accounting you usually must obtain the prior consent of the Treasury Department (Internal Revenue Service).

Other Records

In addition to bookkeeping records, it is generally advisable to maintain other records, particularly after your business is started. For example, for each customer it is advisable to keep a customer's file where you can place all the data pertaining to that account, in addition to an accounts receivable ledger card that shows sales, collections, and other accounting data. In such a file you would include information as to who does the purchasing for the customer, a general description of your customer's business, terms of sale, how he came to be a customer, etc.

Likewise, it would be practical for you to keep a file for each product you manufacture, listing information such as the names and addresses of various suppliers of materials that make up the basic product, prices quoted and paid, etc. Any formula used for making the product should be kept in this file unless you want this to be kept secret: in that case you should put it under lock and key or in your safety deposit box. This file would also be a good place to put any newspaper or magazine articles about your particular products or about products similar to yours made by competitors.

What kind of records should be used for bookkeeping purposes? Other than those prepared on accounting machines or by computer, which most crafts- **23** men are not ready to use when they first start business, there are two types to select from: loose-leaf columnar journals and ledger sheets, or bound journals and ledgers. Naturally the loose-leaf sheets are more flexible. Bound books are generally pre-numbered in numerical sequence, and should you make errors or spoil certain pages and thus have to rewrite part of your books, you cannot destroy a page or pages without breaking the sequence of page numbers and perhaps breaking the binding. Of course, you can always cross out an entry or entries, but this tends to make a messy set of books. Then too, if you are using a limited number of sheets, loose-leaf is also better, for at the end of the accounting year you can file that year's journals and ledgers away for future reference.

Of course, you can make use of a computer, either through the service department of a manufacturer of computers, or through other individual computer service companies. While you still are responsible for preparing the basic records (e.g., check book coded by account number for each disbursement, completed sales invoices, details of deposits, etc.) the computer service will take those records and prepare your various journals, ledgers, trial balances and statements, depending on what you want and are willing to pay for. However, until a reasonable volume of transactions can be maintained, records prepared by hand will generally prove to be more economical.

Filing

Let us offer here a few tips on filing. Do not heap invoices or paid bills in a receptacle without regard to date or items. Rather, set up a filing system so that paid invoices may be readily referred to. There are many filing systems in use, but the two generally used are alphabetical by vendor or product, and by accounts classification or number. Under the latter system similar items would be grouped under appropriate headings such as Purchases, Rent, Repairs, Supplies, and the like.

Copies of all tax returns which you prepare and file should be retained for future possible use. They will be of great help in the preparation of future tax returns, and they will be particularly needed if you later must file a claim for a refund. They may also be helpful to the executor of your estate, or for review in case you should be called upon for an audit by the Internal Revenue Service.

3 ACCOUNTING FOR INCOME

Before we go into the subject of accounting for income, remember that it is a good business policy to deposit as soon as possible all receipts, whether cash or checks, in a commercial or checking bank account, preferably a separate one for your business. In this way you not only will have a complete record of your transactions, but there will also be less chance that such items will be lost or stolen.

Income for the average craftsman who is starting in business will generally be in the form of cash or a check received from the sale of his work, and in the beginning the only basic record he will need will be his check book. In this particular book he will list all income received as a result of his work. Included with the amount of the deposit should be such other data as the name of the customer who made the payment, an invoice number or date, and, should the payment be for less than the full amount, a notation to that effect. Later such details will serve as a basis for entries into what is known as a cash receipts journal.

Sometimes you will have other supporting data in regard to a sale, such as voucher stubs which may be attached to a customer's check, a letter which may have accompanied the check, or a copy of your sales invoice. If you have any of these, they together with a copy of your deposit ticket should be put in a large envelope or folder that is clearly marked as to date of deposit and amount and filed away for future reference. It is sometimes surprising how much you can forget in the space of six months or a year.

Cash Receipts Journal

As we have already stated, the best way to record income is to use a cash receipts journal. This is a lined book with as many columns as necessary for ease in recording and summarizing your transactions. The number of columns that you use will be based primarily on the volume and type of your transactions. For example, if there are just a few and you sell for cash only, then you could have the following columnar headings in the cash receipts journal:

Date	Description	Cash Deposited	Net Cash	Sales	Sales Tax	Other Account	Amount
		1	2	3	4	5	6

To illustrate the use of such a journal, let us consider the following situation:

1. On September 1 you start your business and invest $500 which you use to open a business checking account.
2. On September 2 you sell a pot you have made for $200.
3. On September 10 you find that you need more cash for the business, so you borrow $300 from your bank, on a 6% note due in 90 days.
4. On September 12 a client asks you to make a special design for $1,000 and gives you a deposit of $250.

Now to record these entries in the cash receipts journal. In accounting, when you design a journal you must consider the possible number of similar entries, and if one type of account is to appear more frequently, then a separate column should be set up for this type of transaction. As Sales should be the more common account, other than Cash, the columnar sheet would thus look like this after recording the entries mentioned above:

Date	Description	Cash Deposited	Net Cash	Sales	Sales Tax	Other Account	Amount
9/1	Investment Capital for Business	$500.00	$500.00			Capital	$500.00
9/2	A. Smith	214.00	214.00	$200.00	$14.00		
9/10	1st Natl. City Bank	300.00	300.00			Notes Payable Bank	300.00
9/12	B. Jones	250.00	250.00			Deposits Customer	250.00
		$1,264.00	$1,264.00	$200.00	$14.00		$1,050.00

You will note that the first two columns are identical, and generally where the amounts in the transaction are few in number the first column may be eliminated. Its only purpose is to enter the amount of the deposit, and it is only needed when a deposit is made up of more than one item.

The cash receipts journal is self-balancing in that the total debits must equal the total credits. As stated earlier, if you increase or add to an asset account, that part of the entry is a debit. Therefore, the net cash column is for debits. If you increase income (sales), capital or a liability account, that part of the entry is a credit, and so the amounts entered in these columns represent credits. Thus we find, after listing and adding these columns, that our debits and credits are equal:

	Debits	Credits
Cash	$1,264.00	
Sales		$ 200.00
Sales Tax Payable		14.00
Other		1,050.00
	$1,264.00	$1,264.00

The amount received from a client in advance of the delivery of your work is usually recorded in a Deposits—Customer account rather than as a sale, because if your product does not satisfactorily comply with the terms of your agreement or contract, the deposit will have to be refunded. Therefore, until such time as an acceptable product is delivered to the customer, the deposit is for all practical purposes a debt owed, and thus a liability.

Sales Invoices

When you make a sale, the customer should be given a receipt or a sales invoice. Such forms can easily be obtained from your local stationery store, or you can have your own forms printed, showing your business name, address and telephone number, with sufficient space to enter information about discounts allowed or other terms of the sale. These forms should be pre-numbered in sequence to record all your sales, whether cash or credit, and the numbers accounted for before entry into what is known as a sales journal.

If you are selling on credit, it will be necessary for you to enter periodically a record of all such sales in a sales journal. To illustrate, let us assume that you have made the following sales in the month of September, your first month in business:

1. On September 2, a pot for $200 to John Jones, on credit. Sales tax: $6.00 (Note: The sales tax here is assumed to be 3%.)
2. On September 5, a bowl for $250 to Alex Smith, on credit. Sales tax: $7.50.
3. On September 6, a plate for $175, for cash, to M. DeGroff. Sales tax: $5.25.
4. On September 10, a vase for $700 to Jessica Hesch, on credit. Sales tax: $21.00.

The first sale would be recorded on your first sales invoice, which will be either number 1 or 100, depending on where you want to start your numbering system. The second sale will be recorded on the next numbered invoice, and so on. These invoices will then be entered into a sales journal, which may be designed as follows:

Date	Sales Inv. #	Customer	Accounts Receivable	Sales	Sales Tax
9/2	1	John Jones	$ 206.00	$ 200.00	$ 6.00
9/5	2	Alex Smith	257.50	250.00	7.50
9/6	3	Cash (M. DeGroff)	180.25	175.00	5.25
9/10	4	Jessica Hesch	721.00	700.00	21.00
			$1,364.75	$1,325.00	$ 39.75

If you are selling on credit, you will have to redesign your cash receipts journal to include a column for Accounts Receivable. In that column you will enter as a debit the amount of your sales (plus tax and other charges) as collected, if collected in full or the amount that is collected, whether it is in part payment or for more than one invoice. In addition you will also eliminate the sales column from the cash receipts journal. You will no longer need to record the sales or sales tax here, since they will be entered in the sales journal.

To support the accuracy of the sales journal, your office copy of the sales invoices should be filed month by month in a binder in numerical sequence. This binder will become a permanent record.

Many businessmen use such a file binder in lieu of a sales journal, since it saves work and is just as effective. If this is done, an adding machine tape is run of the amounts shown on each sales invoice, and the total of this tape would be the same as the total for Accounts Receivable in a sales journal. Of course, if you have to contend with a sales tax, then two other totals must be determined—one for the amount of the actual sales and one for the amount of the sales tax. The total of the sales invoice will be the amount to be debited to Accounts Receivable, the total of the actual sales will be credited to Sales, and the total of the sales tax will be credited to Sales Tax Payable.

If you plan to have your sales invoices printed, then you will have to decide how many copies of each invoice you will need. Your printer should be able to give you some helpful advice in this regard. Generally five copies are standard: the first, or original, for the customer; the second, for use only if the customer is delinquent in making a payment; the third, for your customer file; the fourth, for your sales journal; the fifth as a record to support your cash receipts journal. Sometimes businessmen prefer to have a different color sheet for each copy, but in the case of a new or small-scale business, this would probably be an unnecessary expense. As a reminder, don't forget to have your invoices numbered in numerical sequence.

If you wish to economize by reducing the number of copies of the sales invoices, a duplicate of your bank deposit ticket could be used instead of the fifth copy which is designed to serve as a back-up record for your cash receipts journal. Simply indicate on the duplicate copy the names of the customers whose checks you are depositing, the amount to be credited to Accounts Receivable, and any other information needed to record the transaction properly in the cash receipts journal.

Sales Taxes

According to the laws of almost every state, the retail seller must charge and collect a sales tax at the rate set by the state or other taxing authority. In many of those states, the retailer is required by law to register with the appropriate taxing authority. At such time he will receive a number which is used on his periodical reports when he remits the tax collected (or that should have been collected). He must also give this number to wholesalers or others from whom he purchases merchandise or materials to be used in making the product he intends to sell.

If someone who purchases your product claims that he is doing so in order to resell it and thus is exempt from paying a sales tax, you must receive from him his "resale" number and indicate this on your invoice together with the fact that the sale was for "resale." This number is generally recorded on what is known as a sales tax exemption letter. In addition, some organizations such as schools and recognized charities may be exempt from paying a sales tax. You should indicate this on your sales invoice and also obtain from them an "exemption letter."

It is important that you keep proper records of the sales tax collected inasmuch as you are subject to an audit by the taxing authorities. The basic records would be the sales invoices which show the tax that was collected, or that the sale was for resale, etc. You will also have an account in the general ledger which will be supported by entries and details shown in your sales journal or cash receipts journal. If you are operating a retail store, another basic record would be your cash register tape. In addition, you should retain a copy of your sales tax return plus your work papers prepared to compile amounts shown on that return. These sales tax returns are generally prepared and filed quarterly.

Since regulations for sales taxes differ from one state to another, you should be sure to consult the local tax regulations of your state in this regard. **29**

Should you make a sale on credit rather than for cash, you should first record some basic facts about the purchaser that will prove his identity and give you reasonable certitude that he will pay for the merchandise on or before the date called for by the terms of the contract—in most cases, that shown on the sales invoice. If the amount is not too large, it should be sufficient for the purchaser to identify himself by showing you his driver's license. The notations you make from his credentials can be used for future reference, or you can obtain from him credit references, suppliers, or others with whom he has been dealing, and then either telephone or write to them for confirmation of his ability to pay. Of course, you should not ship or deliver the merchandise until you are sure of his credit standing.

If the customer has received the merchandise but has not paid by the due date, then you must take steps to remind him that his account is past due, either by sending him a statement or a copy of the invoice, or by a telephone call, followed by another notification a short time later if payment has still not been received. Thereafter, you could employ the services of a collection agency who, for a fee, will try to collect the amount due. Generally, if they fail, you will pay no fee. Of course, the last resort is always the courts.

When your customer offers to pay by check, you should require some identification unless his credit has been established from previous sales. The safest way is to check whether his signature on the check corresponds with that on his driver's license and then noting any pertinent facts from the license such as his address. Should the check be returned by the bank because of insufficient funds, you can use the data obtained from the license for collection purposes. It would also be advisable to obtain his telephone number at the time you record the other data.

Nowadays many customers like to use credit cards, and if you plan to sell at retail you may have to become familiar with the procedures for handling such cards when making a sale and also how to collect your money afterward.

You should make it a habit to deposit promptly the money received from your sales, particularly when checks are involved. If you delay too long, the customer may not have sufficient money in his checking account to cover the amount by the time you try to cash it, and when the check bounces both you and he will have unnecessary problems. There is also the chance that you may misplace the check or lose it completely, thus causing you the embarrassment of requesting another check and giving him the problem not only of issuing a new check but of requesting the bank to put a stop-payment order on the original. Finally, it is simply a good business practice to make your deposits promptly so that the money will be in your account ready for use.

4 ACCOUNTING FOR EXPENSES

Aside from minor items out of petty cash, you should pay for everything by check. In this way your record of payment will be complete, since the endorsement on the check furnishes proof of payment. If someone other than the payee has cashed the check, then the bank who made the payment will in most instances become liable. Any endorsement other than that of the payee should be discovered by you when you reconcile your bank statement with your books, and any error on the bank's part should be called to their attention immediately.

Voucher Checks

If possible, you should use what is known as a voucher check when making payments. This particular type of check, which can usually be obtained from your bank or local printer, provides a space where you can indicate just what you are paying for, the date of the vendor's invoice, the invoice number, and amount of the invoice. Upon its receipt the vendor will know exactly what the check covers and the cancelled check returned to you will be an excellent record for tax and business purposes. A sample voucher check is shown here:

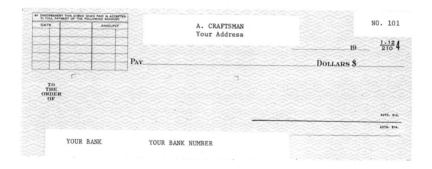

You will note that on this sample check two places have been provided for signatures. This is sometimes done for better internal control. However, in most instances when only a small business is involved the checks will provide for just one signature.

Verifying Invoices

It is very important that every invoice you receive from a vendor clearly indicates what he is charging for. Thus you will have definite proof that the purchase was for something that you use or need for your business—in other words, what federal tax regulations refer to as "an ordinary, necessary business expense."

Upon receipt of an invoice you should check to see that what you are being billed for was received and in the correct quantity, that it arrived in good condition, and that the price charged for each item was that agreed upon when the order was placed. You should then check carefully to ascertain that no mistakes were made by the vendor in arriving at the total amount to be paid. Some bills are made out by computers; others are made out by individuals. In either case, errors are not an uncommon occurrence.

If the material received is to be used in the production end of your business and is therefore exempt from a sales tax according to the laws of your state, make sure that none has been charged.

In order to show that the various steps listed above were taken, many businessmen use a voucher stamp and affix this to each invoice. As each step is completed it is initialed, together with the date it is done. This is important in helping you to decide if the invoice to be paid is in order.

A sample voucher stamp follows:

Acct.	*Account*
No.	*Title*
....	....
....	....
Approved by ....
Material received ....
Extensions checked ....
Date Paid	Check # ....

Petty Cash Fund

In the case of small expenditures—i.e., purchases at local stores for $10 or less—you should obtain a cash sales slip or receipt which gives some general indication of what you purchased, so that if the tax authorities should question you, you can show that the expenditure was for essential business purposes. These small expenditures would be paid for out of petty cash.

If you cannot get a receipt or sales slip for some expenditures such as carfare, then you should prepare what is known as a petty cash voucher, to be signed by the person receiving the money as reimbursement. This particular form may be obtained from your local stationer. In addition, whenever you purchase stamps for business purposes, you should write out your order on a petty cash voucher and have the post office clerk stamp your order to indicate what you have purchased.

To keep track of your small expenditures, you may wish to use a "petty cash book." If so, each time that money is taken from the petty cash fund, you would make an entry to record how much money was withdrawn and what the expenditure was for.

You will also have to determine the minimum amount of money you wish to keep in the petty cash fund so that it can be replenished when necessary. Some businessmen prefer simply to total the withdrawal slips every week and then to put that amount back in the fund, thus starting each week with the same cash total. If you follow this method, you can avoid the problem of keeping a petty cash book. However, in the long run, such a book will be of help to you in keeping a more accurate record of your expenditures for tax purposes. (If more convenient, this procedure can be done monthly rather than weekly.)

If you have several people working for you, the petty cash fund should be entrusted to one employee who would be responsible for keeping a record of the signed receipts for various disbursements and for seeing that all the money is accounted for either in cash or in petty cash slips.

Cost Accounting

Another part of your records that deserves most careful scrutiny is that of cost accounting. Whether you produce or manufacture one or many items, it is absolutely essential for you to know what your approximate production costs are for each, both for tax purposes and to enable you to determine what price to charge so that you can earn a fair profit. As a start, at least keep a separate columnar sheet for each product or type of product and enter the elements of your cost. Naturally such information could also be used to determine the inventory value of any items unsold at the end of your accounting and tax year.

Entertainment Expenses

If your tax return should be audited by the Internal Revenue Service, one deduction that is generally called into question is that claimed for entertainment expenses (sometimes called "promotional expenses"). The federal tax regulations are rather specific as to what can be deducted and what records you need to substantiate your claim. In general, Section 274 of the Internal Revenue Code states that no deduction shall be allowed for any expenditure for travel, entertainment, or a gift unless the taxpayer substantiates the following elements for each such expenditure:

1. the amount spent;
2. the time and place of travel or entertainment (or use of a facility for entertainment), or the date and description of a gift;
3. the business purpose involved;
4. the business relationship to the taxpayer of each person who is entertained, uses an entertainment facility, or receives a gift.

Unless you can show that the entertainment expense is directly related to your business as a necessary and ordinary expense, any deduction taken will be disallowed in an audit of your return. By "directly related to your business," we mean that as a result of your entertainment expense you expect to derive business income or some other business benefit in the future. Moreover, it cannot be purely a good will visit. You must talk about business while dining or entertaining, or such discussion must occur just prior or subsequent to the actual entertainment. If you meet all these provisions, you can also deduct costs of entertaining at home.

In case of a tax audit you must be able to substantiate each expenditure, and where the expenditure is over $25 you must provide a receipt or cancelled check in support of your claim. If it is allowed, however, in most cases the Internal Revenue Service will deduct a portion of the total expenditure for dining as representing that which you would have normally spent for that meal if you were alone.

To keep track of your entertainment expenses, a regular diary will be acceptable as long as you record in the diary (on the proper day) the name of the person or persons with whom you have your business lunch or dinner, the place, and the business purpose—in other words, who, when, where, and why. Even if you do not expect to do much in the entertainment field, it is a good policy to purchase a diary so that it will be available should you need it.

Booklets specifically designed to allow you to record these types of expenses are sold by business stationers. They generally resemble the following:

TRAVEL AND ENTERTAINMENT EXPENSE RECORD

Date   *Amount*

Transportation: Train, bus, cab, car rental, etc. ....
Tips ....
Meals: Breakfast ....
       Lunch ....
       Dinner ....
Hotel—Lodging ....
Entertainment ....
Misc: Telephone, stationery, etc. ....
     Total ....

EXPLANATION OF TRAVEL EXPENSES
AWAY FROM HOME ON BUSINESS

Number of Days Away	Away From To	Means of Travel	Business Purposes (Reason for Travel)

ENTERTAINMENT

Date	Persons Entertained Name, Business or Occupation, etc.	Place Where Entertained	Type of Entertainment	Reason for Entertainment i.e., Benefit Sought or Obtained

IF BUSINESS NOT DISCUSSED WHILE ENTERTAINING
SPECIFY THE FOLLOWING INFORMATION

Date	Persons Discussing Business Preceding or Following Entertainment (name, occupation, etc.)	What Discussed	Place	Duration

Inventories

Inventories may be an important part of your business assets, and you should know something about how their values are computed, since the Internal Revenue Service regulations state that they must be used to determine your taxable income or loss if they are an income-determining factor. In addition, these regulations state that the method of valuing inventories may not be changed without the permission of the Internal Revenue Service. The subject is covered in detail in the next chapter.

Recording Cash Disbursements

Just what method you should use for recording disbursements depends on your type of business, the volume of transactions, and your clerical or bookkeeping help. Generally at the beginning the easiest way is to keep a cash disbursements journal together with a file of unpaid bills or invoices. Such a record should have as many columns as are necessary for ease in recording and summarizing your transactions. The following will serve as an example:

Date	Vendor	Check No.	Net Cash	Materials	Expenses Acct.	Amt.	Other Acct.	Amt.
9/1	Company A	1001	$186.20	$190.00	—	—	Cash disc.	$ (3.80)
9/2	Company B	1002	175.00	—	Rent	$175.00		
9/3	Company C	1003	147.00	—			Furn. & Fix.	150.00
							Cash disc.	(3.00)
9/4	Craftsman A	1004	100.00				Drawing	100.00
			$608.20	$190.00		$175.00		$243.20

This type of journal or columnar sheet comes in varying sizes and number of columns and may be purchased from any stationery store that sells business supplies.

Recording in the cash disbursements journal simply involves taking the data from the check book where each stub should show the amount paid, any discount taken, and the account to be charged, based on the information shown on the invoice. If you have a numbered chart of accounts, you can simply use the account number instead of the name of the account on both the check stub and in the cash disbursements journal.

If the invoice to be paid is subject to a cash discount—usually expressed by the words 2% 10 days, 30 days net—you are entitled to deduct this amount when you pay on or before 10 days from the billing date. When recording the entry in the cash disbursements journal, the amount of such discount should be deducted from the face amount of the invoice or shown separately as a credit, specified as a "cash discount."

Voucher Register

When your volume of transactions increases to the point that a bookkeeping record of your outstanding obligations or bills is advisable, you should set up what is called a "voucher register." This particular record would essentially show the details of expenses or expenditures that previously were recorded in the cash disbursements journal. Here the columnar headings would be similar to those in the cash disbursements journal, except that the Net Cash column would be replaced with one entitled "Accounts Payable," and the Check Number column would be replaced by one entitled "Paid On" to record the date on which the debt was paid. If such a register is maintained, you will know at all times the exact amount you owe, simply by noting the bills for which there is no entry under the column "Paid On."

A sample voucher register, with entries similar to those shown in the cash disbursements journal, follows:

Inv. Date	Vendor	Paid On	Accts. Payable	Materials	Expenses Acct.	Amt.	Other Acct.	Amt.
8/24	Company A	9/1	$190.	$190				
8/26	Company B	9/2	175.		Rent	$175		
8/28	Company C	9/3	150.				Furn. & Fix.	$150
8/30	Stationer		82.		Stat.	82.		
			$597.	$190.		$257.		$150

37

In such a register, the total of the three last columns should equal that under "Accounts Payable," following the principle of double entry bookkeeping wherein total debits equal total credits. As this particular record shows, the bills for this period total $597, and what is currently owed is $82, since that invoice is the only one that is listed as unpaid, there being no entry under the "Paid On" column.

At the end of each accounting period, the amounts shown in this voucher register must be posted to their respective accounts in the general ledger. For example, the total of the Accounts Payable column would be posted as a credit to that account in the general ledger, whereas the total for the Materials column would be posted as a debit. The other columns would be posted as debits directly to their respective accounts.

Since the voucher register replaces the columns for distribution of expenses and expenditures formerly shown in the cash disbursements journal we must consider what our new cash disbursements journal would be like. A suggested format follows:

Date Paid	Check Number	Net Cash	Accounts Payable	Other Accounts	Amount
9/1	1001	$186.20	$190.00	Cash discount	$ (3.80)
9/2	1002	175.00	175.00		
9/3	1003	147.00	150.00	Cash discount	(3.00)
9/4	1004	100.00		Drawing	100.00
		$608.20	$515.00		$ 93.20

Here again you will see that the total debits ($515.00 + $93.20) equal the total credits ($608.20), as must occur under the double entry bookkeeping system. The posting of these items to the general ledger would follow the procedure mentioned under voucher register posting.

Employee Records

If you decide to employ others to assist you, you should start a personnel record for each individual. This file should include copies of letters to the employee as well as any correspondence concerning checks you have made of his references, prior employment, etc. Data regarding his starting salary and any pay increases also belong in the file. Make sure that any application for employment form which you use does not request the prospective employee to show his race, color, creed, or age, since this would be in violation of the anti-discrimination laws.

Besides the personnel file you will need to keep wage records. To do so is an absolute necessity, for you will need them to prepare your quarterly payroll tax returns and the annual wage reports to each employee (W-2 Form), as well as for a possible audit of your payroll tax returns or your workmen's compensation insurance policy. These records should be posted periodically from your cash disbursements book which would be redesigned to show additional columns for the various taxes withheld and a column for gross salaries or wages paid.

The wage record may simply be a card or a sheet for each employee, and it should be balanced periodically—every month or at least at the end of each quarter. The totals from these sheets or cards should agree with the entries in the general ledger for salaries and for taxes withheld.

A form of an employee record card is as follows:

RECORD OF EARNINGS AND EMPLOYMENT

RECORD OF EMPLOYMENT AND EARNINGS

NAME		S. S. NO.				19	
ADDRESS		WORK	FIRST QUARTER	TOTAL EARNINGS	O. A. B.	W. T.	
CITY		DEPT.	SECOND QUARTER				
SINGLE OR MARRIED		SALARY	THIRD QUARTER				
NUMBER OF DEPENDENTS		DATE STARTED	FOURTH QUARTER				
WITHHOLDING STATUS		DATE LEFT	TOTAL AMOUNT				
REMARKS		REASON					

FIRST QUARTER							THIRD QUARTER						
WEEK ENDING	TOTAL WAGES	DEDUCTIONS			TOTAL	NET PAYMENT	WEEK ENDING	TOTAL WAGES	DEDUCTIONS			TOTAL	NET PAYMENT
		FEDERAL O. A. B.	WITH-HOLDING TAX						FEDERAL O. A. B.	WITH-HOLDING TAX			
TOTAL							TOTAL						

SECOND QUARTER	FOURTH QUARTER

These or similar cards may be purchased at any commercial stationers and come in many designs, all of them containing the basic information shown above. The columnar headings for various deductions can be changed to fit your particular situation. Naturally the other quarters would also be shown on the card.

You must also obtain from each new employee a signed Federal Employee's Withholding Allowance Certificate (W-4 Form) which may be obtained from your local Internal Revenue Service office. This form gives you the authority to deduct federal withholding from the employee. Should there be a change in the employee's status, he must complete a new W-4 Form.

If you make payments of $600 or more during the year to an individual other than a full-time employee from whom you withhold taxes, you will have to file a 1099 Form. In order to complete this form you will have to obtain the person's Social Security or Employee Identification number. After all the necessary 1099 Forms have been prepared, you will summarize their totals on Form 1096, to which the 1099's are attached, and then file this material with the Internal Revenue Service center in your area within two months after the end of the year.

As a final note on this subject, when you first engage employees, you must obtain an SS-4 Form from your local Internal Revenue Service office, complete it and mail it back to them. You will then receive an Employer's Identification number which is to be used in filing payroll and other tax returns.

Capital Expenditures

If you should purchase equipment, machinery, etc., which is of value and has a life of more than one year, good accounting practices and the tax regulations state that you cannot charge the cost as a current expense of doing business. Rather, that cost must be written off over the life of the asset through depreciation. However, as a practical matter, expenditures for separate items of equipment costing less than $15 each may be written off as an expense at the time of purchase rather than through depreciation. (see chapter 6).

In addition to your bookkeeping records, you should maintain what is sometimes called a fixed asset ledger. The purpose of this ledger is to record the purchases and sales of all capital expenditures for insurance purposes and also in case of fire or theft or another casualty. The details shown on a sheet filed in such a ledger would include information such as a description of the machine or equipment, the serial number, from whom it was purchased, the name of the manufacturer, whether it was new or second-hand, its location in the plant or office, the invoice cost, freight and installation costs if any, and the depreciation period or rate.

5 TAXES

If you are in business, taxes are unavoidable. Just what taxes will be involved will depend on where your business is located and how much profit you make. Specific information about the taxes that are in effect in your area can be readily obtained from your local tax office. Also, you must keep in mind that the tax laws are in a constant state of change and this book is only intended to give the reader a basic understanding of many complicated areas.

For example, if you live in New York City and do business there as a sole proprietor and employ people, here is a list of taxes you may pay, or collect and remit, aside from sales taxes (and, if you own property, real estate taxes):

1. Federal Income Tax, Form 1040 and Schedule C plus Schedule SE (1040) for self-employment tax (better known as the Social Security tax).
2. New York State Income Tax, Form 201 or 208, depending on whether you are single or married.
3. New York City Income Tax, Form 201 or 208, similar to that for New York State.
4. Unincorporated Business Tax for New York State and for New York City under certain conditions.
5. Federal Income Tax withheld from employees' salaries, and Federal Old Age Benefits, better known as Social Security, on Form 941.
6. New York State Withholding.
7. New York City Withholding.
8. Commercial Rent Tax.
9. Occupancy Tax.
10. New York State Unemployment Tax.
11. Federal Unemployment Tax.

Withholding and Unemployment Taxes

Withholding taxes—federal, state, and city—are payable either by making semi-monthly or monthly deposits or by filing quarterly or semi-annual returns, depending on the amount and type of tax you withhold from your employees. You may obtain specific filing instructions from the respective federal, state and city taxing authorities.

In addition, at the end of the year you must also prepare a W-2 Form for each of your employees and for the Internal Revenue Service, as well as similar forms for New York State and New York City.

The commercial rent tax is payable either quarterly or annually, based on   **41** the amount of rent that you pay, whereas the occupancy tax is payable annually.

If your business is in New York State and you have an employee, you are subject to New York State unemployment tax on the first $4,200 of his salary or wages in any one year. This tax is not deducted from your employee's salary or wages. Before you start paying this tax you must register with the New York State Department of Labor on a special form, 1A 100, in order to obtain an employer registration number. Upon registration they will assign you a rate of tax, generally 2.7%, which may or may not be adjusted at the beginning of each year based on your experience rating. These tax reports are due quarterly. As with all taxes, there are many rules and regulations, and these will be explained in the handbook that the Labor Department furnishes to you on registration.

You are subject to federal unemployment tax if during the current or preceding calendar year you (1) paid wages of $1,500 or more in any calendar quarter, or (2) had one or more employees for some portion of at least one day during each of 20 different calendar weeks. The 20 weeks do not have to be consecutive. Individuals on vacation and sick leave are counted as employees in determining your status. These conditions apply to unemployment tax but not to social security tax or withholding of income tax.

The federal unemployment tax is imposed on you as an employer; it must not be collected or deducted from the wages of your employees. The rate for 1974 and 1975 is 3.2% on the first $4,200 of wages paid to each employee during the calendar year. You may receive credit for up to 2.7% of the wages for state unemployment taxes you pay or for having been granted a favorable experience rate by the state. For this reason your net federal liability may be as low as 0.5% of taxable wages for 1974 and 1975. Form 940 is designed to take these credits into account.

Meals, lodging, and other payments in kind are subject to federal unemployment tax just as are wages paid in cash.

Additional information on depositing or filing requirements or determining your tax liability may be found in Circular E, obtainable from the Internal Revenue Service and the instructions to Form 940, the annual return.

Estimated Tax Payments

As a businessman operating as a sole proprietor, you may draw money against profits, but you are not paid a wage or salary for your services. Thus there are no taxes withheld from the money drawn. However, since federal and most other income taxes are on a pay-as-you-go basis, you must estimate and declare your income taxes for the year and pay your estimated tax quarterly on special forms provided.

In regard to filing, you will not need to do so unless one of the following is applicable to you: (1) your estimated tax is $100 or more for the year; (2) your estimated gross income will include more than $500 in income not subject to withholding (this would include profit from your business, interest on savings, etc.); (3) you are married and entitled to file a joint return with your spouse who receives no wages and your estimated income for the year exceeds $20,000; (4) you are married and entitled to file a joint return, have an estimated individual gross income in excess of $10,000, and both you and your spouse receive wages for the year; (5) you are married but not entitled to file a joint return and have an estimated gross income exceeding $5,000.

Don't forget that if, in addition to your private business, you are also employed, you may eliminate the filing of a declaration of an estimated tax, by having additional amounts withheld from your wages. An estimated tax is simply the amount you believe that your income tax, including the self-employment tax, will exceed any expected withholding of tax from your wages.

Such estimated taxes are payable on or before April 15, June 15, September 15, and January 15 of the following year. If there should be a significant change in your estimated tax, either up or down, you can amend your declaration on any of the dates shown. If you fail to pay an estimated tax, or if you underpay, there will be a penalty. The basis for determining the amount of this penalty and how to avoid incurring it is described in the instructions to the form supplied by the Internal Revenue Service.

Federal Form 1040ES, "Declaration of Estimated Tax," also includes a worksheet to help you with this problem. There are similar declarations required by other taxing authorities—e.g., New York State and New York City—and thus you will have to check out the regulations of your particular locality.

Preparation of Your Tax Form

The comments that follow are concerned specifically with the preparation of Schedule C, Form 1040, which is the federal tax form to be filed by a sole proprietor or individual in business. In most instances, however, they will also apply to the owner of a corporation or for a partnership return.

As mentioned in Chapter 1, all income is taxable unless expressly exempt by law.

Income that you receive from your avocation (business) is taxable and must be reported on Schedule C, Form 1040. This would include net income from the sales of your product (sales less costs), or any other income that may be related to your business operations. For example, if you rent part of your business property, your rental income must be reported. Likewise, if you have

43

any recoveries of bad debts in prior years under the specific charge-off method, these should also be included. Refunds of taxes deducted in prior years should be reported as income and not offset against the current year's tax expense.

However, when you are in business you can deduct from your taxable income all "ordinary and necessary expenses" that you incur even when they exceed your income and thus show a loss. Some examples of expenses that you can deduct are:

- Cost of goods purchased for production or resale, except that which is unsold and properly included in inventory at the end of taxable year, as explained later
- Supplies
- Repairs
- Auto expenses, as explained later
- Local transportation expenses
- Advertising and other selling costs, including the cost of photographing your work
- Insurance premiums for fire, storms, theft, and other losses
- Entertainment (see Chapter 4 for comments and for sample forms)
- Business gifts
- Expenses of exhibitions
- Bad debts, if you are on an accrual basis of bookkeeping
- Books, pamphlets, and magazines used in your profession
- Casualty and theft losses
- Wages paid to employees
- Interest on business loans
- Professional society dues
- Rent (full amount unless you work at home, in which case a proportionate amount of the rent you pay)
- Telephone (your business phone expenses, or that part of your home phone expenses chargeable to business, plus those calls that you make from pay stations for business)
- Depreciation (see Chapter 6)
- Work clothing (when required by your profession and not adaptable to general wear, plus cost of cleaning)
- Heat, light, power
- Commissions
- Taxes (payroll or others pertaining to business, but not federal income taxes)
- Accounting and bookkeeping expenses
- Agent expense

- Legal expense
- Bank charges
- Cost of cleaning your studio, shop, or office
- Experimental and research expenses
- Maintenance (full amount if you own the premises, or that amount for which you are liable if you rent)
- Stationery (invoice forms, letterheads, cards, etc.)
- Parking meter deposits (while on business)
- Postage
- Travel and transportation expenses (see below)
- Cost of preparing professional tax returns
- Educational expenses (amounts you spend for your education in connection with your profession. Travel and transportation in connection with such education are also deductible when it is customary for other established members of your profession to undertake such education to maintain or improve skills required in your profession. A statement should be attached to your return, explaining the deduction and showing the relationship of the education to your profession.)

Travel and Transportation Expenses

You may deduct travel and transportation expenses incurred in carrying on your profession, provided that they are directly attributable to your profession and are ordinary and necessary in the conduct of it. Accurate records should be maintained of all traveling and transportation expenses which you incur. (See Chapter 4 for sample forms.) Attach a statement to your return explaining in detail the expenses claimed. If you deduct traveling expenses, your statement should show:

- the nature of your profession;
- the number of days away from home on your profession;
- the amount expended for meals and lodging;
- the amount of other expenses connected with your travel.

Meals and lodging during travel are deductible provided that they are not lavish or extravagant. The extent to which they are lavish or extravagant depends on the facts and circumstances in each case.

Travel expenses are those incurred when you are away from home overnight on business. The principal traveling expenses are:

- Meals and lodging expense
- Transportation expenses, including automobile expenses to the extent that **45**

they are attributable to professional trips
- Cost of transporting necessary baggage, samples, display materials, etc.
- Tips connected with the above

Since traveling expenses are deductible only if incurred while away from home overnight, the meaning of the terms "home" and "overnight" are important. For travel expense purposes, "home" refers to your principal place of business, regardless of where you maintain your family residence. Thus, there may be occasions when, according to tax regulations, you are traveling away from home even while you are working in the same city in which you and your family live.

The term "home" is not limited to a particular building or property, but includes the entire city or general area in which your business is located.

In regard to the term "overnight," you may be away from home overnight if your professional activities require you to be absent from your "tax home" for a period which is substantially longer than an ordinary day's work and if, when away, it is reasonable for you to need and to obtain sleep or rest in order to meet the requirements of your professional demands. In this respect, you need not be away from your tax home for an entire 24-hour day or throughout the hours from dusk to dawn. (It should be noted, however, that the courts have not always accepted this definition, especially when the taxpayer takes up employment at a new location for a definite period.)

Cab fares and other transportation expenses incurred in getting from one client to another, or from one place of business to another, are deductible.

You may deduct travel expenses which you incur in attending a convention, conference, workshop or exhibition if you can actually show that your attendance is directly related to your profession and will benefit or advance the interests of that profession.

Transportation expenses are deductible if they are directly attributable to the actual conduct of your profession. It is not necessary that they be incurred while you are traveling away from home overnight, but they do not include meals and lodging. Included in transportation expenses are fares for air, train, bus, taxi, etc., and the costs of operating and maintaining your automobile.

Commuting expenses incurred between your residence and your usual place of business are not deductible, regardless of the distance involved. However, the costs of traveling from your principal place of work to the place where you practice your profession, other than your home, are deductible. For example, Jones takes a bus from his house to his full-time job. After work, he takes a bus to a shop where he makes furniture as a sideline. When he leaves the shop he takes the bus home. The tax regulations permit him to deduct the fare in traveling from his full-time job to his sideline profession. If he takes a cab instead of a bus, he can deduct the cab fare; he is not required to use the cheaper form of transportation to get the deduction. If he uses his car instead of public transportation, he can deduct the car expenses attributable to the drive between his full-time job and the shop. However, he cannot deduct the fare or car expenses traveling from his house to his full-time job, or the fare or car expenses traveling from the shop to his house. These are personal commutation expenses and are not deductible.

Professional and Personal Expenses

You must be careful to distinguish between professional or business expenses and personal expenses. You may deduct some of your personal expenses (medical, casualty loss, interest on mortgage, etc.) only when you choose to itemize your personal deductions, and not when you take the standard deduction which is 15% of adjusted gross income (16% for 1975 only), not to exceed $2,000 ($1,000 in the case of a married person filing a separate return). (For 1975 *only* it is $2,300 for single, $2,600 for married filing jointly and surviving spouses and $1,300 for married filing separately.) If your adjusted gross income is less than $10,000, the standard deduction is automatically considered in the table you use to determine your tax. The tax regulations assert that you are entitled to the 15% standard deduction (16% for 1975 only), or what is termed a low-income allowance designed to provide a tax-free allowance for low-income taxpayers. This is designed to remove many taxpayers from the tax rolls and may amount to as much as $1,300 ($1,900 for married filing jointly in 1975). It is also built into the tax table so that no separate figuring is required.

When you qualify your avocation as a profession and you file as a sole proprietor or individual, you will deduct all your professional expenses on a separate Schedule C, Form 1040, whether you itemize or not. (Itemized personal deductions are deducted on Schedule A, Form 1040.)

As we have mentioned, however, if your personal deductions are less than 15% (higher in 1975, see earlier paragraph) of your adjusted gross income (not to exceed $2,000), claiming the standard deduction will give you a lower tax.

We will offer here two examples. Don't forget that when your adjusted gross income is less than $10,000, the standard deduction and/or the low-income allowance are built into the table you use to determine your tax.

Example A:

In 1974 Brown had a salary of $9,000. He incurred travel expenses of $500 while away from home, while his personal deductions for interest, medical expenses and other costs totaled $600.

Gross income (salary)	$9,000
Less: Travel expenses	500
Adjusted gross income	$8,500
Less: Standard deduction (15%* of $8,500)	1,275
Taxable income	$7,225

*16% for 1975. See earlier paragraph.

Brown took the standard deduction, since his actual deductions were less than $600.

Example B:

In 1974 Green, a crafts instructor, had a salary of $7,000. He earned $2,000 from his sideline profession of weaving. Interest and taxes on his home and other personal deductions amounted to $250, and he paid $300 interest on a professional loan. His other professional expenses totaled $1,400.

Gross income:

Salary		$7,000	
Professional income	$2,000		
Less:			
Professional expenses	$1,400		
Interest on business loans	300		
		1,700	
Business income			300
Adjusted gross income			$7,300
Less: Standard deduction (15%* of $7,300)			1,095
Taxable income			$6,205

*16% for 1975. See earlier paragraph.

For 1974 Green takes the standard deduction, $1,095 ($7,300 x 15%), since it is greater than his actual itemized personal deductions of $250. If his itemized deductions had exceeded $1,095 he would itemize them rather than take the standard 15% deduction. You will note that he can deduct his professional expenses and professional loan interest from his business income on Schedule C and also take the standard deduction. In this way he deducts $2,795, although his actual expenses are only $1,950.

Another advantage that the professional enjoys can be shown by the following example. Suppose that a $300 rug you wove is stolen. If you are a professional you can deduct the entire $300 on Schedule C as a theft loss. However, if you are a non-professional, you can list theft losses as a personal deduction on Form 1040 only if you itemize deductions. In addition, the personal deduction for theft losses is only allowed for a loss over $100; thus you can only deduct $200 ($300 minus $100). The professional can deduct the entire $300, whether or not he itemizes his personal deductions.

You are not allowed to deduct most of your personal expenses even when you itemize. For example, you may not deduct expenditures made for the purposes of promoting your personal prestige or establishing your professional reputation, nor can you deduct expenditures for travel, entertainment, etc., made with a view of establishing yourself in a profession. Moreover, when you itemize, you cannot deduct depreciation and repairs on your car or house. You can, however, deduct certain taxes and interest payments. As a professional you can deduct depreciation and repairs (as well as taxes, interest, etc.) applicable to your business operation, whether or not you itemize.

Suppose, for example, that you use your car and house partly for professional and partly for personal purposes. You can deduct the portion of your expenses (including depreciation, repairs, etc.) allocable to your profession. To get the deduction, however, you must clearly distinguish between personal and professional use.

Deducting Auto Expenses

When you use your automobile *exclusively* for your profession, your entire cost is deductible. However, when you use your auto for both personal and professional purposes, you must apportion your expenses between personal and professional travel. As a crafts teacher, suppose that you drive your car 20,000 miles during the year. You drive 8,000 miles for professional purposes and 12,000 miles for personal purposes. Thus only 40% of the total cost of operating your car may be claimed as a professional expense. Of course, in case of an audit, you must be able to substantiate such claims.

In computing your total auto expenses, figure the amounts you spend for gas, oil, tolls, parking and other costs, including garage rent, storage, repairs, insurance, etc. You also can deduct the proportionate share of depreciation. (See Chapter 6 for a discussion of depreciation available only as a business expense.)

It should be pointed out that if you take a 100% allowance on your automobile and your return is audited by IRS you can expect the agent to disallow a portion as personal expense.

Instead of keeping records of your actual auto costs, the law allows you to use a simplified or standard method to figure your costs. All you need to know is your business mileage, and then you can deduct, as an auto expense, **49**

15 cents per mile for the first 15,000 miles and 10 cents per mile thereafter instead of actual operating costs and depreciation, except in the case of a fully depreciated automobile, in which case the deduction is limited to 10 cents a mile. You can use whichever method of computation is of greatest financial benefit to you. Moreover, you are not required to use the same method each year. However, if you use the itemized rather than the simplified method, you must keep proper records such as checks, vouchers, receipted bills, etc.

To use an example, let us suppose that you drive your car 20,000 miles a year—4,000 miles for professional purposes, and 16,000 miles for personal purposes. Your actual expenses, including depreciation, for gasoline, gas taxes, oil, repairs, etc., total $1,875. Since one-fifth (4,000 out of a total of 20,000 miles) of your use is for your profession, you may deduct $375 (1/5 of $1,875), or you may deduct $600, using the simplified method (4,000 miles x 15 cents per mile). Naturally you would choose the method giving the larger deduction. (Note: When you use the simplified method, you cannot deduct depreciation, since that is included in the standard mileage rate.)

Some auto expenses are deductible as personal deductions whether or not you are a professional, but only if you itemize your deductions instead of using the standard method. Such expenses would include state gasoline taxes, interest on auto loans, and casualty and theft losses (except the first $100) not compensated by insurance. As a professional, however, you can deduct part of all of these expenses even though you choose the standard deduction, because now professional expenses are involved. When you use your car partly for professional and partly for personal purposes, you can, as we have previously noted, deduct the portion of your professional costs for gasoline taxes, interest on auto loans, etc. The non-professional who does not itemize his deductions cannot deduct these expenses.

Deducting Household Expenses

When you use part of your house for your profession, you can deduct that part of your household expenses attributable to professional use. You may use any reasonable method of allocating the cost of telephone, repairs, fire insurance, depreciation, taxes, light, heat, painting, etc. When you rent your house or apartment, you may allocate the portion of the rent attributable to your professional activities. One commonly used method of allocating expenses is based on the ratio of the number of rooms used to pursue your profession to the total number of rooms in your house. However, make sure that a specific room or part of a room you use for work is not normally used by other members of the family. To illustrate, suppose that a craftsman rents a three-room apartment; he creates jewelry in one room and lives in the other two rooms. A reasonable apportionment is the ratio of the number of rooms used for his work to the total number of rooms in the apartment. Thus he would deduct as a professional expense 1/3 of the rent paid on that apartment, plus 1/3 of the other expenses such as heat, light, etc. See the following example, where $590 is deductible as a professional expense:

	Total	1/3 Professional	2/3 Personal
Rent	$1,500	$500	$1,000
Heat	180	60	120
Electricity	90	30	60
Total	$1,770	$590	$1,180

To use another example, suppose that a craftsman owns a five-room house for which he paid $25,000 ($20,000 for the building, $5,000 for the land). The house has a useful life of 25 years (salvage value is zero). He uses one room, or 1/5th, for making pottery. Here is how he deducts his expenses:

	Total		Itemized Personal Deductions	Deductible on Schedule C as Professional Expenses
Taxes	$ 500		$ 400	$ 100
Interest	400		320	80
Depreciation	160	(see below)	not deductible	160
Repairs	400		not deductible	80
	$1,460		$ 720	$ 420

Depreciation:

Building Cost	1/5th of Cost or Basis	Useful life	Depreciation*
$20,000	$4,000	25 years	$160

*Using straight line method—see Chapter 6 on depreciation.

The $720 of expenses in the column "Itemized Personal Deductions" is deductible only if the craftsman itemizes his deductions. Repairs allocated to personal use of the house are non-deductible personal expenses. No depreciation deduction is allowed for the part of the house used for personal purposes. The craftsman deducts $420 on Schedule C as professional expenses whether or not he itemizes his personal deductions.

Inventory

If you make several articles during the year that remain unsold at the end of the tax year, then you have what is termed an "inventory," and this should be considered in arriving at your taxable income. The tax regulations say in effect that inventories are required where the production, purchase or sale of merchandise is an income-producing factor in the business.

If an inventory is necessary, it should be not only for the finished goods or products, but also for the work that you may have started but did not finish (called work in process) and for the materials which have been acquired to be used in making the finished product which are still on hand and have not been used (called raw materials).

There are two ways to approach inventories and it depends on your need to know at any time what you have available for use. One approach would be to keep what is known as a book inventory record, which would show purchases, sales (at cost) and balance or inventory, at end. The latter would then be verified by the taking of a physical inventory and checking this against the quantities that you show in your book inventory. The other approach would be to take a physical inventory only. If you do this you have nothing to check against but your own knowledge of what should be there.

As a general rule, the average small business should take only physical inventories as a means of arriving at taxable income. The main thing to remember is to be consistent in your method from year to year.

Depending on what is involved, the determination of an inventory may be by count, weight, or any means that is fairly accurate, and the value should be determined in accordance with a method acceptable to the tax authorities.

According to the Internal Revenue Service, almost any method for valuing inventory may be used as long as it is consistent and clearly reflects the taxable income. However, tax regulations state in effect that certain methods are prohibited. Some of these are: (1) establishing a reserve for price changes or an estimated depreciation in value, (2) excluding or omitting a portion or portions of inventory that has value, and (3) adding to the inventory any goods en route or in transit when title has not passed to you.

If you must use an inventory in computing your taxable income, then you must also use the accrual basis of accounting for purchases and sales.

It may be advisable to consider adopting the accrual method of accounting at the time you start your business even if you do not expect to have an inventory at the end of your first tax year. The reason is simple. If you do and subsequently you must use an inventory to compute your taxable income, then you will not have to apply for permission to change, since you will have already adopted the accrual basis of accounting.

Once a method of inventory pricing is adopted and you desire to change, then you must file an application on Form 3115 within 90 days after the start of the taxable year for which the change is desired. The method that you decide on must be used for the entire inventory.

The inventory value or cost of finished goods or the finished product ready for sale should include the cost of raw materials and supplies consumed in making the product, the amount expended for labor in its production (including any overtime), and overhead or indirect expenses; however, you cannot include any selling and administrative expenses.

Let us offer here a brief description and examples of two methods of inventory pricing:

1. *Lower of Cost or Market.* The bid price generally is considered the market at the date of inventory and must be determined for each article and then compared with the cost for that article. The lower figure is taken for inventory purposes. An example, based on specific identification of items in inventory, would be if you purchased twenty-five pounds of clay at 38 cents per pound on November 25, 1974, and twenty-five pounds on December 10, 1974 at 36 cents per pound. The market value (bid price) of clay on December 31, 1974 was 37 cents per pound. If all of the clay were on hand at the end of the year, you would value the first purchase at market or 37 cents per pound, and the second at cost or 36 cents per pound. However, identification of items in inventory may not always be practical to apply, so you may wish to use a moving average method, or some other acceptable method.

However, as the American Institute of Certified Public Accountants has stated in Bulletin 29 of the Committee of Accounting Procedure, (a) market should not exceed the net realizable value (estimated selling price in the ordinary course of business less reasonably predictable costs of completion and disposal), and (b) market should not be less than the net realizable value reduced by an allowance for an approximately normal profit margin.

2. *Last In, First Out.* (referred to as *Lifo*) To use this method you must have the approval of the Internal Revenue Service. The valuation of the inventory is at cost, with the materials or items in the inventory considered to be the last ones purchased. This method may be used for all of the items in the inventory or for specific items. However, the Internal Revenue Service may require its

53

use for other items or for similar goods in another business of the taxpayer if it is deemed necessary to clearly reflect income.

From a practical standpoint, craftsmen will not have serious inventory problems when they first start out in business. However, as time goes on a problem may develop, and then you should investigate to find the one system that is best for your business.

Other Savings

One final thought about saving on taxes: Should your spouse or children assist you in your business, it is advisable to pay them for their services even if they don't request it. In a state like New York where they have an income tax, it may be better tax-wise for your wife or husband to file a separate return so as to get the benefit of a lower tax, since New York doesn't have separate tax rates for married persons filing joint returns. As in all tax savings plans, a quick computation will tell you just how much you can save, depending on what your taxable income is. However, unless you are operating as a corporation, present tax regulations do not permit you to deduct the social security tax on what you pay your spouse as salary or wages.

6 DEPRECIATION AND INVESTMENT CREDIT

Depreciation is deductible when you are in business. As a professional you can deduct depreciation on all property used in your activities. For example, a potter can deduct depreciation on his kiln. He also can deduct depreciation on his car and home if he has used them professionally. If one-third of their use is professional, he deducts one-third of the depreciation.

Depreciation Deduction

What is the depreciation deduction? The cost of machinery, equipment, buildings, trucks, office furniture, copyrights, patents, and other property with a useful life of more than one year is a capital expenditure and may not be deducted as an expense in the year of purchase. However, in lieu thereof, you may deduct, or pro-rate each year, a portion of such expenditures as a reasonable amount for depreciation to take care of exhaustion, wear and tear, and obsolescence of property used in your profession. The depreciation deduction allows you to recover your investment over the useful life of the property. What is reasonable depends on the facts known at the end of the year for which the allowance is figured.

What property qualifies for the depreciation deduction? The property must have a limited and determinable useful life and must be used in your profession. You may not take depreciation on your home, its furnishings, your auto, or other items which you use only for personal or pleasure purposes.

When you use property for both professional and personal purposes, only that part of the depreciation which is allocable to your professional use may be deducted. For example, if you use your car one-third of the time for professional purposes and your car depreciates $600 this year, your depreciation deduction is $200 (1/3 of $600).

Other Facts To Remember about Depreciation

Ownership for Less Than a Full Year. When you acquire property during the year, regular depreciation is allowable for only that part of the year in which you own the asset, but the full amount of additional first-year depreciation (discussed later) may be deducted.

Depreciation Allowed or Allowable. You should claim the proper amount of your depreciation deduction for each year. If, in prior years, you failed to deduct the reasonable depreciation, you may not deduct the unclaimed depreciation of prior years in the current or any later tax year.

Depreciation Cannot Exceed Cost. The aggregate of the depreciation allowed or allowable cannot exceed the cost of the property less its salvage value (as defined later).

Useful Life. The first step in figuring depreciation is to determine the estimated useful life of each asset to be depreciated. The useful life of an asset depends upon how long you expect to use it, its age when acquired, your policy as to repairs, upkeep and replacement, and other conditions. There is no average useful life which is applicable to all situations. Average useful life is determined on the basis of your particular operating conditions, experience, and replacement policy. The estimated useful life of an asset is not necessarily the useful life inherent in the asset, but the period over which the asset may reasonably be expected to be useful in your profession.

The useful life prescribed by the Internal Revenue Service as a guide for depreciation purposes applies to all assets used in a particular profession or business rather than to individual assets.

However, you may claim useful lives longer or shorter than those given by the Internal Revenue Service if they are consistent with your retirement or replacement practices.

For more information as to useful lives and other guidelines for depreciation, obtain a free copy of Internal Revenue Service Publication No. 534, "Tax Information on Depreciation," from the District Director of the Internal Revenue Service office in your state.

Salvage Value. This is the amount, determined at the time of acquisition, which you estimate will be realized upon the sale or other disposition of the asset when it is retired from service. The estimated salvage value must be deducted from the cost of the asset in determining the annual depreciation, unless you use the declining balance method (discussed later). You may not depreciate an asset below salvage value.

The determination of salvage value depends upon the way you generally operate. If it is your policy to dispose of assets when they are still in good operating condition, the salvage value may represent a large part of the original cost of the asset. However, if you customarily use an asset until its useful life has been substantially exhausted, the salvage value may represent no more than junk value.

If you acquire personal property (other than livestock) with a useful life of three years or more, you may reduce its salvage value by any amount up to 10% of the cost or other basis of the property. If the salvage value is less than 10% of the cost or other basis, you may disregard it. For example, suppose that you purchase a station wagon for your personal use on January 5, 1973, for $4,500. On January 5, 1974, you convert the station wagon to business use, and at that time it has an estimated useful life of four years, an estimated salvage value of $500, and a basis for depreciation of $3,000 (fair market value). You choose the straight-line method of depreciation and decide that you want to reduce the salvage value.

Basis for depreciation		$3,000
Less: Salvage value	$500	
Reduction in salvage value 10% of $3,000	300	200
Amount to be depreciated over the remaining useful life		$2,800

Where To Deduct Depreciation. If you are filing as a sole proprietor, depreciation on professional property is deductible on a separate Schedule C which is attached to your 1040 Form. If you are filing as a corporation or partnership, then special provision is made on the tax forms applicable to those types of organizations for depreciation.

Additional First-Year Depreciation. You may choose to deduct 20 percent of the cost of qualifying property (subject to the dollar limitations defined below) in addition to your regular depreciation. You may not use salvage value in computing this deduction. The following facts about first-year depreciation are important for you to know:

1. *When Allowable.* You may take this deduction only in the first year for which a depreciation deduction is allowable on the property. This is ordinarily the year in which the property is acquired.

2. *Qualifying Property.* This is (a) tangible personal property, (b) new or used, (c) not real property, (d) having a useful life of at least six years from the date of acquisition. Tangible personal property includes assets used in the operation of your profession, such as kilns, looms, machinery, office equipment, individual air conditioning units, etc. It does not include wiring in a building, plumbing systems, central heating or central air conditioning machinery, pipes, ducts, or other items which are structural components of a building or other permanent structure. To qualify the property must be purchased for use in your profession, and, as we have stated, it may be new or used.

Buildings, their components, real estate, land, and intangible personal property such as patents do not qualify for the deduction, nor does property if acquired by gift or inheritance. Moreover, the additional allowance is not allowed on property purchased or otherwise acquired from certain related parties as defined in the regulations.

3. *Limitation.* The cost of the property on which you may take this additional allowance is limited to $10,000 on a separate return and $20,000 on a joint return. For example, if during the year you purchased $30,000 worth of qualifying property, you may deduct 20 percent of only $10,000 on a separate return, or 20 percent of only $20,000 on a joint return. You may select the items, and the portion of their costs on which you wish to claim the additional allowance.

4. *The Election.* You must make the election separately for each year for which you claim additional first-year depreciation, and it must be made on your income tax return for the year to which such election applies. The election is made by showing, as a separate item in the depreciation section on the tax return, the additional first-year depreciation claimed for each piece of qualifying property you select.

5. *Records.* You should keep records which permit specific identification of the property for which the additional first-year depreciation is claimed and which show how and from whom such property was acquired.

6. *Computation of Deduction.* Unlike ordinary depreciation, the additional first-year depreciation deduction is determined without regard to salvage value and is allowed in full even though the property is acquired during the year. Ordinary depreciation is then computed on your cost of the property, after deducting the additional first-year depreciation deduction, and less salvage value, if required.

Methods of Figuring Ordinary Depreciation

In figuring ordinary depreciation, you may use any reasonable method which is applied consistently. The three methods most generally used are: (1) straight line, (2) declining balance, and (3) sum of the years—digits.

1. *Straight Line Method.* In this system, the cost of the property, less salvage value, is generally deducted in equal annual amounts over the period of its estimated useful life. You can determine the depreciation for each year by dividing the cost of the property, less salvage value, by the remaining useful life of the property.

2. *Declining Balance Method.* In this system, the amount of depreciation you take each year is subtracted from the cost or other basis of the property before computing next year's depreciation, so that the same depreciation rate applies to a smaller or declining balance each year. Thus, a larger depreciation deduction is taken for the first year you use this method, and a gradually

smaller deduction is taken in each succeeding year. Within limits a depreciation rate is used which is greater than the rate which would be used under the straight line method.

Under some circumstances you may use a rate which is twice as great as the rate which would be proper under the straight line method. Under other circumstances you are limited to a rate which is one and one-half times as great as the rate you would use under the straight line method.

Twice the straight line rate is the maximum rate which may be used to compute depreciation under this method on any of the following tangible property:

(a) Property having a useful life of three years or more which you acquire new after December 31, 1953.

(b) Property having a useful life of three years or more which is constructed, reconstructed, or erected by you after December 31, 1953.

One and one-half times the straight line rate is the maximum rate you can use under the declining balance method on tangible property which does not meet the above qualifications, provided that such a method results in a reasonable allowance for depreciation. This includes new and used property acquired before January 1, 1954 and used property acquired after December 31, 1953. This method may be elected in the first return filed in which depreciation is sustained on the property.

Salvage value is not deducted from the cost of your property in determining the annual depreciation allowance under this method. You must not, however, depreciate your property below reasonable salvage value.

3. *Sum of the Years—Digits Method.* In this system, you apply a different fraction each year to your cost of the property less its salvage value. The denominator (or bottom) of the fraction is the total of the numbers representing the years of useful life of the property. Thus, if the useful life is five years the denominator is 15 ($1 + 2 + 3 + 4 + 5 = 15$). The numerator or top of the fraction is the number of years of life remaining at the beginning of the year for which the computation is made. Thus, if the useful life is five years, the fraction to be applied to the cost minus salvage, to figure depreciation for the first year, is 5/15, the fraction for the second year is 4/15, and so on. Note, however, that depreciation on the sum of the years—digits method is allowed only on the property which meets the requirements for twice the straight line rate explained above under the declining balance method.

Comparison of the Three Methods

Suppose a new kiln costing $2,625 and having an estimated life of ten years is bought on January 2. The salvage value is estimated to be $100. You elect to claim additional first-year depreciation on the kiln since it is tangible personal property having a life over six years. Your deduction is 20% of the cost of $2,625 (disregarding salvage value), or $525.

Under the straight line method, the ordinary depreciation is $200, computed as follows: Deduct the salvage value of $100 and the first-year depreciation of $525 from $2,625 (cost of kiln), leaving $2,000. Then divide $2,000 by ten (the number of years of useful life), to arrive at the annual depreciation of $200.

Under the declining balance method, the annual ordinary depreciation may not exceed 20%, that is, twice the straight line rate of 10% in the example above. The ordinary depreciation the first year is $420—20% of $2,625 (cost) less $525 (additional first-year depreciation). The depreciation for the second year is $336 (20% of $1,680, the unrecovered cost).

Under the sum of the years—digits method, the ordinary depreciation would be $363.64 the first year. This is 10/55ths of $2,000 (cost of $2,625 less $525 additional first-year depreciation and $100 salvage value). The numerator of the fraction represents the ten years of useful life remaining at the beginning of the year, and the denominator of the fraction is the sum of the numbers one through ten. The depreciation for the second year would be 9/55ths of $2,000, for the third year, it would be 8/55ths of $2,000 and so on.

A detailed comparison of the three methods follows:

Annual depreciation

Year	Straight line 10%	20% declining balance	Sum of the years—digits
First year additional depreciation	$ 525.00	$ 525.00	$ 525.00
First year ordinary depreciation	200.00	420.00	363.64
Total depreciation first year	$ 725.00	$ 945.00	$ 888.64
Second year depreciation	200.00	336.00	327.27
Third year depreciation	200.00	268.80	290.91
Fourth year depreciation	200.00	215.04	254.55
Fifth year depreciation	200.00	172.03	218.18
Sixth year depreciation	200.00	137.63	181.82
Seventh year depreciation	200.00	110.10	145.45
Eighth year depreciation	200.00	88.08	109.09
Ninth year depreciation	200.00	70.46	72.73
Tenth year depreciation	200.00	56.37	36.36
Total	$2,525.00	$2,399.51	$2,525.00
60 Salvage value or unrecovered cost	$ 100.00	$ 225.49	$ 100.00

Generally, any change in your method of computing depreciation is a change in your method of accounting, and the consent of the Internal Revenue Service is required except as discussed below. A request for a change should be made on Form 3115, available from your Internal Revenue Service office, and must be filed within 90 days after the beginning of the tax year in which you desire to make such a change. However, permission is not required to change:

(a) from the declining balance method to the straight line method, if such change is not prohibited by a written agreement as to useful life and depreciation rates;
(b) from either the declining balance method or the sum of the years—digits method to the straight line method, or from the declining balance method to the sum of the years—digits method where asset depreciation ranges are used;
(c) to a method of depreciation permitted or required for property that is residential rental property.

To make any of the above changes, however, you must attach to your return, for the tax year in which the change is made, a statement showing the date of acquisition of the property, the cost or other basis, the amount recovered through depreciation and other allowances, the estimated salvage value, the character of the property, the estimated remaining useful life of the property, and other pertinent information.

Investment Credit

When you acquire for use in your profession any new or used depreciable tangible personal property with a useful life of at least three years, you may be able to reduce your tax liability by 7% (10% for 1975/1976*) of the purchase price of the qualifying property depending on its useful life. Machinery and equipment are the principal types of property eligible for this credit—for example, kilns, casting equipment, etc. In order to claim this credit you must complete and file Form 3468 with your Federal income tax return. You should also check your state and local income tax regulations, since they may also provide an "investment credit." On the back of Form 3468 there are general instructions which state briefly who must file (any individual, corporation, etc., but not partnerships and small business corporations, since credit is claimed by the partners or shareholders), when the credit is allowed, and the property covered.

There is a dollar limitation on used property, which in general is the amount of such property, but not in excess of $50,000 ($100,000 for 1975/76*). If a husband and wife file separate returns, each may claim only up to $25,000, unless one of them has no qualifying used property, in which case the other may claim up to $50,000.

As we have stated, if you are qualified for a credit it will reduce your tax liability, but the amount of this credit does not reduce the basis of the property to be used for depreciation purposes.

Recapture Rules

If you dispose of an asset before the expiration of the useful life on which the credit was computed, you must recompute the investment subject to the credit, using as the useful life the asset period that you actually held it. The investment credit must then be recomputed. If the recomputed credit is less than the credit you actually used to reduce your tax (either in the year the asset was placed in service, or in any carryback or carryover year), you must add to your tax liability, for the year in which the asset is disposed of, any excess of any credit you originally used over the recomputed credit.

In redetermining the credit for an asset disposed of on or after August 16, 1971, use the new useful life categories (3-5-7 years) applicable under the Revenue Act of 1971. If the asset was disposed of before August 16, 1971, use the useful life categories (4-6-8 years) applicable before that act was passed. For example, suppose that on February 1, 1966 you acquired for $6,000 a machine having an estimated useful life of 8 years, and that on your 1966 return you claimed the full credit of $420 against a tax liability of $1,000. However, on July 1, 1971, you sold the machine. Since you held the machine more than 4 years but less than 6 years, your recomputed credit is $140, and you must add $280 to your 1971 tax, the excess of the original credit claimed in 1966 over the recomputed credit.

If the recomputed credit is more than the credit you have actually used to reduce your tax (either in the year the asset was placed in service or in the carryback or carryover year), you decrease the unused credit difference between the original credit available and the recomputed credit.

---

* Under the Tax Reduction Act of 1975 you, as a taxpayer, are entitled to a 10% investment credit for qualified property acquired and placed in service after January 21, 1975 and before January 1, 1977. Self-constructed property will also qualify for the 10% credit if you complete it after January 21, 1975, but only to the extent of the property basis attributable to construction after that date and before January 1, 1977.

The same Tax Reduction Act provides that you can purchase $100,000 (increased from $50,000) of used property in the same period. If a husband and wife file separately the dollar limitation is $50,000 up from $25,000.

62

In addition to the rule on disposing of assets, there are others that apply to property traded, replacement property and casualty and theft losses. There is also a limitation on the amount of credit to be claimed and provisions for carryback and carryover of unsued credits. All of this is explained on the back of Form 3468. If you still want further information, you can write to the District Director of the Internal Revenue Service office in your state and ask for a free copy of Publication 572, "Tax Information on Investment Credits."

Gain from the Disposition of Depreciable Property

The depreciation allowable for an asset may affect the gain or loss computations upon the sale or other disposition of depreciable property.

The gain on certain dispositions of depreciation property used in your business or held for the production of rents or royalties may be treated as a capital gain. However, all or part of the gain on a disposition of depreciable property may be treated as ordinary income under certain rules. In this case, the part of your gain that is not ordinary income under these rules may be considered for capital gain treatment. Note also that different rules apply to personal property and to real property in determining what part, if any, of the gain on disposition is ordinary income.

You must keep permanent records of the facts necessary to determine the depreciation allowed or allowable on your depreciable property (after 1961 on personal property and after 1963 on real property) for determining the gain to be reported as ordinary income. This includes dates of acquisition, cost or other basis, depreciation, and all other adjustments that affect the basis.

For further information on this subject you can obtain free from the Internal Revenue Service office in your state, Publication 511, entitled "Sales and Other Disposition of Depreciable Property."

7 OTHER HELPFUL FACTS

In connection with taxes, there are other points to keep in mind. One is the retention of your business and personal records for possible tax examinations and other needs. The basic rule applicable to federal income tax returns is that the Internal Revenue Service may examine your tax return within the statute of limitations for that particular return. Usually this is three years from the date the return was filed, or two years from the date the tax was paid, whichever occurs later. This would mean that if you filed your return for the calendar year 1972 on or before April 15, 1973 you should retain your records, as explained later, until at least April 15, 1976. However, the statute of limitation is six years in the case of a substantial omission of a material portion of income.

Maintenance of Records

You should file your records in a place where they are safe from damage and easily accessible. These records would consist of everything you need to support an item of income or a deduction appearing on your return. Such would include bank statements and cancelled checks; books, records, or work sheets used in preparing your return; copies of wage or salary withholding statements (W-2 Forms); Form 1099 for income earned but not subject to withholding; brokers' statements, purchases and sales advice; invoices or bills supporting deductions, etc.

In property transactions, sometimes the basis of new or replacement property is determined by reference to the basis of the old property. Records of transactions relating to the basis of property should be kept for as long as they are material in determining the basis of the original or replacement property. Also, new legislation will occasionally give tax benefits to a taxpayer if he can prove from his records of transactions in prior years that he is so entitled.

Copies of tax returns that you have filed should be kept as part of your records, since they may be helpful in preparing future returns.

Income Averaging

While three years from the date of filing is the basic rule for retaining records applicable to your tax returns, you must also consider such returns for income averaging, which is permitted under the present Internal Revenue Service regulations.

The income averaging method permits a part of an unusually large amount of taxable income to be taxed in lower brackets, thus resulting in a reduction of the over-all amount of tax due.

You may choose this method of computing your tax if you are an eligible individual, as discussed below, and your average income for the previous year was more than $3,000. Your average income will generally be the amount by which your adjusted taxable income exceeds 30% of your total base period income (the sum of your taxable incomes, with certain adjustments) for the four immediately preceding tax years. Thus, if you win a lottery, have substantial capital gains, or just have a great year in your chosen craft, your income may be high enough to average.

To offer a simple example, suppose that Craftsman A, who is an eligible individual (as defined later), is a calendar year taxpayer who has never been married and whose only source of income is and has been his salary and income from his profession. Last year he had a taxable income of $20,000, which is the amount on line 48 of his 1040 Form. (In this case this is his adjusted taxable income for last year, his computation year.)

Then on Schedule G he enters this and his taxable incomes for his four base period years, as follows: $7,000 in 1970, $8,000 in 1971, $4,000 in 1972, and $5,000 in 1973. The sum of these amounts to $24,000, 30% of which is $7,200.

Thus Craftsman A's averagable income for last year is $12,800, determined by subtracting $7,200 (30% of his total base period income) from $20,000 (his adjusted taxable income for 1974). Since this is over $3,000, he may use the income averaging method. Still using Schedule G, he then computes his tax as follows:

(1)	30% of total base period income (*.30 x $24,000*)	$7,200.00
(2)	1/5 of averagable income (*1/5 x $12,800*)	2,560.00
(3)	Sum of items (1) and (2)	$9,760.00
(4)	Tax on sum of items (1) and (2) (*tax on 9,760*)	$2,030.00
(5)	Tax on 30% of total base period income (*tax on $7,200*)	1,398.00
(6)	Tax on 1/5 of averagable income (*item 4 minus item 5*)	632.00
(7)	Tax on 4/5 of averagable income (*item 4 x item 6*)	$2,528.00
(8)	Tax for 1974 (*sum of items 4 and 7*)	$4,558.00

Under the regular method, the tax on $20,000 taxable income is $5,230. Thus he saves $672 by using the income averaging method.

Eligibility for Income Averaging

You are eligible to compute your tax under the income averaging method only if you (and your spouse, if you file a joint return for the computation year) meet two tests. The first test relates to citizenship or residence, and the second test relates to the percentage of your support attributable to you (and your spouse). This method is available only to individuals.

To be eligible to compute your tax under the income averaging method, you must have been either a citizen or a resident of the United States throughout your computation year and your base period years. Moreover, you must have furnished 50% or more of your support during each of your four base period years. If you file a joint return, both you and your spouse must meet the support test. However, there are certain other exceptions that are not applicable to most persons, and if you desire more information it can be obtained free in Publication No. 506 from the Internal Revenue Service office in your state.

Retirement: Keogh Tax Plan

As a taxpayer, you should consider setting up what is called a Keogh tax plan. This section of the tax regulations permits you as an individual to invest up to 15% of your earnings from self-employment activities, with a maximum of $7,500, in any program that has been approved by the Internal Revenue Service. Thus, if you are self-employed as a craftsman, either full- or part-time, and have earnings from your craft or another self-employment income (freelance writer, fees for speeches, etc.) you can set aside at the present time in such a plan up to 15% of these earnings with a maximum of $7,500. Suppose that you earn $6,000 for the year and you decide to contribute to such a plan. You would complete the necessary arrangements with any of the many banks, mutual funds, or insurance companies offering such a plan before the end of your next tax year. At the time you prepare your tax return, you would complete the proper schedule. If you decide to set aside 15%, you would then deduct $900 from your income and thus pay tax on $5,100, instead of on $6,000. The amount you save at that time will depend on the tax bracket you are in. If it is 30%, it would mean a savings at this time of $270.

Naturally, if you withdraw these funds before your retirement, they will be taxed at the time of withdrawal; otherwise they will be taxed at the time you retire. However, on your retirement you would generally take the money out over a period of years, and this fact, coupled with the likelihood that your tax bracket should be lower with less income, means that you will probably have a net savings. In addition, any income dividends, or capital gains earned on the funds set aside would not be taxed until they are withdrawn.

You can continue to allot or contribute money to such a plan until you retire. However, if you have employees, you must cover all full-time employees who have worked for you for three or more years. If you have not been in business for at least three years when you establish such a plan for yourself, you must cover full-time employees who have as much service as you have, three years or more. A full-time employee is one who normally works more than 1000 hours during a twelve month period.

Social Security

Outside of the possibility of setting up your own retirement fund as permitted under this Keogh tax plan, most self-employed craftsmen can only look forward to collecting social security.

However, in order to collect you must pay, and your contributions for social security benefits are as follows: If you are an employee, you pay 5.85% of the first $13,200 ($14,100 in 1975) of your wages, and your employer pays a similar amount. However, when you are in business as a craftsman—in other words, self-employed—you pay 7.9% of the first $13,200 in 1974 ($14,100 in 1975) of your income from your business. This tax is in addition to your federal income tax. Moreover, even if all your income, including business income, is not sufficient for you to have to pay an income tax, you still must pay a social security tax if your "self-employed" business income is more than $400. Should your employer withhold all or part of your social security tax, this amount would be taken into consideration when you prepare Schedule SE (Computation of Social Security Self-Employment Tax).

At the present time, you can retire and collect social security benefits at age 65 or 62, or before then if you become disabled. Naturally, if you retire before 65, your benefits will not be as large. Your local Social Security office will furnish charts to show you the differences.

After you retire and start collecting social security, you can still work and earn money. When you reach the age of 72, you can earn as much as you like with no penalty. However, at the present time (1974) you can only earn up to $2,400 per year until you are 72 without having any benefits withheld. Such earnings are from work of any kind but do not include income from savings, investments, pensions, insurance, etc. However, if your earnings in any one calendar year exceed $2,400, you will lose $1 in benefits for every $2 in earnings over $2,400. On the other hand, you can get full benefits for any month in which you do not earn more than $200 in wages and you do not perform substantial services in self-employment. According to the Social Security Administration, "the decision as to whether you are performing substantial services in self-employment depends on the time you devote to your business, the kind of services you perform, how your services compare with those you performed in past years, and other circumstances of your particular case. The amount you earn without having any benefits withheld will increase automatically in future years as the level of average wages rises."

There are many other rules and regulations pertaining to social security, such as payments for disability and to certain dependents of a worker who has died, lump sum payments made on a worker's death, etc. A visit to your Social Security office may be advisable for information as to your possible benefits.

Extensions for Filing Tax Returns

If you find that for some reason you cannot prepare and file your federal income tax return on time, you do not necessarily have a problem. For most taxpayers, both individuals and corporations, the Internal Revenue Service has provided a system wherein by completing a certain form you can automatically obtain an extension of two months as an individual and three months as a corporation. For example, an individual's return for the year ending December 31 would normally be due on April 15, but by properly completing and filing Form 4868, you can automatically get an extension to June 15. The corresponding form for corporations is Form 7004. At the time you file for the extension, you must pay an amount, or balance, based on what you consider you owe for the year. Any unpaid balance after you finally determine your tax will bear interest at 6 percent from the original due date of the return.

If you, as an individual, cannot file by the time the first extension runs out —June 15 in the example above—you can file for a further extension by filing Form 2688. On this particular form you must state the reason why you cannot file, and if it is reasonable you should be granted a further extension of about 90 days. A similar provision is possible for a corporation through Form 7005. Partnerships can also request an extension by completing and filing Form 2758.

Estate and Gift Taxes

In addition to income taxes and social security taxes, a craftsman should also have some knowledge of federal estate and gift taxes. (Some states have also adopted estate and gift tax regulations, but the comments here apply only to federal regulations.)

The first essential in this regard is that you should have a will prepared and completed, because this is the only way you can be certain that your property —your own work, money, and other items on hand at the time of your death

—will be distributed according to your wishes.

The mechanics of preparing a will generally means sitting down with a lawyer and letting him know your desires so that he can help you to draw up a good will. Making a will can be an involved process, and it is best done by some person, preferably a lawyer, who knows about such things as marital deductions, etc.

Naturally you will not personally pay estate taxes, since this will be done after you are dead and no longer in command of your property. However, a good will might reduce the tax burden on those to whom you leave your estate.

If while you are alive you should wish to give some property, etc. to your children, grandchildren, or others (except a recognized charitable organization), you may be liable for a federal gift tax. The Internal Revenue Service regulations state that gifts to any person, other than a charity, in any taxable year may be tax-free for the first $3,000 of the value of such gifts. Value doesn't mean your cost, but the fair market value of the gift at the time it was made. If you are married and your spouse joins you in making a gift, then the total tax-free amount to any one person is $6,000.

In addition to what was said above, each individual has a specific exemption of $30,000 which may be used in whole or in part in any one year. The spouse also has a similar exemption, and so the total here would be $60,000 for man and wife.

To use a specific example, suppose that an unmarried craftsman gives his father a gift in 1972 which has a fair market value of $4,000. After deducting his yearly exclusion of $3,000, this would leave $1,000 to be charged against his specific exemption of $30,000. Then in 1973 he makes another gift, this time for $5,000, and this less his yearly exclusion of $3,000 would leave $2,000 to be charged against his specific exemption. In 1974 he makes another gift of $35,000 and again applies his yearly exclusion of $3,000, leaving a taxable gift of $32,000. However, should he elect to apply this against the remaining balance of his specific exemption—$30,000 less $1,000 (1972), less $2,000 (1973), or $27,000—he would have a gift tax to pay on $5,000 ($32,000 less $27,000). From this point on all gifts will be taxed at their fair market value, since his specific exemption has been used up. Obviously, the tax rates increase as the amount of your taxable gifts increase, but they are still lower than the rates for estate tax purposes.

If you do make gifts, these are reported quarterly to the Internal Revenue Service on Form 709. There are also certain rules relating to the sale of gifts by the recipients, but these are far too complex to cover in a book of this scope.

Other Helpful Hints

If you have jewelry, life insurance policies, stock certificates, a will, savings bank books, or other valuable papers, you should have a safe deposit box for their protection that is accessible to you and preferably one other person.

Particularly as your business begins to grow, it would be advisable for you to have a budget so that you can project your probable income and expenses for the next quarter of the year or longer. Unless you are experienced in such work, you will need outside help to do this.

Another factor that you as a businessman should keep in mind is to make your money work. Many people have the habit of letting excess funds lie in a checking account when those funds could be earning interest in a savings account. Just what constitutes excess funds will be more apparent to you if you have prepared a simple cash budget.

Donating Your Works to Charity

In most instances when property is donated to charity, the donor is allowed a deduction based on the fair market value of the property. However, under the present regulations, you as a craftsman can only deduct the actual cost of materials used to complete the work which is being donated. The tax regulations formerly allowed a deduction based on the fair market value, and there has been growing support for a return to the former law, since the present one is truly inequitable.

The following example should make this clear. If you sold a bowl to someone for $200 and its value later increased to $500, the owner could donate this bowl to a recognized charitable organization and claim a deduction of $500. However, if you were to donate a similar bowl that you had made, all you could deduct would be the cost of the materials and nothing more—not even something for the time it took you to make the work.

Scholarship and Fellowship Grants

Whether scholarship and fellowship grants are taxable or excludable from your gross income is subject to certain limitations. To be eligible for this inclusion the payment must be made primarily for your education and training, and not (1) to compensate you for present, past, or future services; or (2) to allow you to pursue studies or research primarily for the grantor's benefit.

If you are a candidate for a degree, such a grant is not taxable unless it requires teaching, research, or other services. In that case, the portion of the amount received that represents salary is taxable. However, if all candidates for a particular degree are required to perform the same services, then such a salary would not be taxable.

If you are not a candidate for a degree and you receive a grant from any of the following: (1) a non-profit organization exempt from tax, (2) a foreign government, (3) an international organization, etc., created or continued under the United Educational and Cultural Exchange Act of 1961, or (4) the United States, or an instrumentality or agency thereof, or a state, a territory, or a possession of the United States, or any political subdivision thereof, or the District of Columbia, then the exclusion allowed is limited in any one taxable year to $300 per month times the number of months in which the grant was received in that year. However, the total amount allowed under any one grant shall not exceed 36 months (whether or not consecutive). As to expenses such as travel, equipment, etc., relative to any grant, these may also be excluded from gross income under certain conditions.

Other Aspects of Taxation

There are many other aspects of taxation that may be of interest to some but not all craftsmen, and if they are applicable to you, it would be worth your while to investigate them more thoroughly. Some of these are:

1. Possible savings of taxes through ownership of your place of residence—house, co-op apartment, etc.—instead of paying rent. Under the present tax regulations, if you itemize your deductions, you are allowed to deduct the amounts paid for real estate taxes and mortgage interest.

2. Educational expenses—see Chapter 5 on taxes.

3. Child care and disabled dependent care. Internal Revenue Service Form 2441, which is used to claim expenses for household and dependent care services, states that if you maintain a household that includes as a member one or more qualifying individuals and itemize your deductions, you may be allowed a deduction for employment-related expenses paid during the taxable year. There are certain conditions that must be met as to adjusted gross income. For example, if you earn less than $18,000 per year, you may deduct up to $400 per month. If you earn more than $18,000, the maximum deduction is reduced. There are other rules, and most of those are on Form 2441.

4. Claiming your child, who is a student, as a dependent. To qualify, your child must be a full-time student during part of some portion of each of

five calendar months a year (not necessarily consecutive) at an educational institution. Even if his earnings are more than $750 (the present amount allowed for dependents), you may still claim him as a dependent. In most cases, if a student or any child under nineteen who is a qualified dependent works and has taxes withheld, he can file a tax return and possibly recoup all or part of such taxes withheld.